THE ANDES

Text by
ENRICO GUIDONI
AND ROBERTO MAGNI

Foreword by
PABLO NERUDA

MONUMENTS OF CIVILIZATION
THE ANDES

GROSSET & DUNLAP
A FILMWAYS COMPANY
Publishers • New York

Frontispiece:
Cerro Sechín: A section of the procession of
figures cut into the stone slabs lining a terrace
wall at this site on Peru's northern coast.

First published in the United States in 1977
by Grosset & Dunlap, Inc., 51 Madison Avenue, New York 10010

English translation copyright © 1977 by Mondadori, Milano-Kodansha,
Tokyo; originally published in Italian under the title *Grandi Monumenti:
Civiltá Andine* copyright © 1972 by Mondadori, Milano-Kodansha, Tokyo; copyright © 1972 by Kodansha Ltd., Tokyo, for the illustrations;
copyright © 1972 by Mondadori, Milano-Kodansha, Tokyo, for the
text.

Library of Congress catalog card number: 74-3643
ISBN   0-448-02025-4
First printing
Printed and bound in Italy by Mondadori, Verona.

Editorial Director
GIULIANA NANNICINI
American Editorial Supervisor
JOHN BOWMAN
Graphics Editor
MAURIZIO TURAZZI

CONTENTS

FOREWORD

Among the invaders of Mexico — obscure peasants, farmhands, convicts, adventurers, and fugitives — was a young soldier named Bernal Diaz del Castillo, who wrote his memoirs some fifty years after the events narrated when he was an elderly municipal counselor in Central America. The immense manuscript was chained to a table in the town hall in Guatemala City, and there it remained, at the disposal of the public. I have seen it with my own eyes, touched it with my own hands. It was an odd sensation to contemplate that great book lying there in chains, written (perhaps by one of the scribes that were so abundant in illiterate Spain) in a clear, precise hand, dictated, for all one knows, by the old soldier from some massive high-backed chair or from the depths of his bed, but in any event, from the depths of truth itself, an incredible truth. Don Bernal had such a good memory, in spite of his age, that he could still reel off the names of all the horses in his story, even the mares that took time out to have foals, and of each and every one of the soldiers who followed Hernán Cortés.

When I read of the deeds of men and gods in the *Odyssey* during my provincial adolescence, or later on when I found my way into the dreamlike, erotic labyrinths of the *Arabian Nights*, I thought that no human being had ever or *could* ever be marked with the preternatural fate of actually stepping foot into such prodigious realms. But I had been mistaken. For an adventure of this very kind fell to the lot of a run-of-the-mill Spanish soldier. The adventure, that is to say, of tumbling all at once from an uncharted star, then rising suddenly to a newly discovered planet inhabited by living gods, infernal music and golden attire. And it also fell to the lot of this man to hand such an experience down to posterity.

It is no secret that all this living splendor was annihilated in blood and darkness. Men and their vestments, temples and profane edifices, gods and kings were all devoured, destroyed, buried. "The Conquest" was a great raging fire. The conquistadors received a vast, resonant world in full creative fever; they left nothing but a planet strewn with ashes. We Latin Americans, descendants of those personalities and heirs of that destruction, have been obliged to excavate, to seek under the various strata of imperial ashes the dazzling gems and colossal fragments of the lost gods. Or we have had to lift our gaze to the heights around us: Here and there some tower of ancient times, issuing forth victorious from the misery of centuries, allows its pride to rear up over the continent. For I myself make a distinction between the subterranean art and the aerial art of the ancient Americans: This is my own individual way of knowing and understanding them.

When I lived in exile in Mexico City, a good many years ago, two strange persons came to see me in the hope of selling certain wares. Under their arms was a voluminous package wrapped in soiled newspapers, and we untied and opened it right there on my table. Inside were many hundreds of golden figurines, perhaps of Chimú, Chibcha, or Chiriqui origin — a treasure that palpitated there on my poor table with the yellow refulgence of the past. Lying there before my eyes were rings, earrings, pectoral ornaments, figures of tiny fish and bizarre birds, abstract stars, circles, lines, discs, and butterflies. The two visitors asked twelve thousand dollars — which I did not have — for all this splendor. They had uncovered it while working on a road between Costa Rica and Panama, and had quickly taken it abroad in an attempt to turn it into ready cash. But they left my house as they had come, with their treasure under their arms, and I have never known what became of all those fishes and butterflies, those lightning bolts of gold.

On another occasion, while I was strolling through the land of the Maya, I stopped at the edge of the forest for a long contemplation of a ceremonial *cenote,* one of those wells whose bottoms of dark, gloomy waters were part of the Mayan mystery. It is said that the ceremony called for the virgins reserved for the gods to be pushed into the wells in mortal sacrifice — young girls clad in gold and turquoises, necklaces, bracelets, and rich robes. A capable entrepreneur of the burgeoning North American empire got the notion in the last century to purchase that land, which appeared to be abandoned, and there he dedicated himself to fishing — down there in those strange deep springs. And the sacred *cenotes* gave him a catch of many pounds of divine jewelry.

This America of ours — Middle and South America — is vast and intricate. Throughout its spiral forms, along its endless rivers, under its mountains or deserts, and even from under the recently constructed streets in the cities, golden memorials of the past come to light day after day. They are tiny anthropomorphic statues of Aztec, Olmec, Quimbaya, Inca, Chancaya, Mochica, Nazca, or Chimú origin. They are millions of vases of baked clay or of wood, enigmatic figures of turquoise or gold, wrought things, woven things. They are millions of ritual, figurative, and abstract masterpieces. They are schools and disciplines, superlative styles, picture-compositions of cruelty, worship, humiliation, sadness, insanity, truth, and joy. They are a whole world palpitating with great bygone festivals tied in with the enigmas of life and death, with the advent of harvests that were to nourish poetry and theogony, in tribute to the resurrection and consecration of spring, to boundless sexual wisdom, to the enjoyment of the land in all its temptations and fruits, or woven into the mystery of absolute silence or possible resurrections. Our museums of Mexico, Guatemala, Colombia, and Peru are full of these figures that were never degraded nor annihilated by their centuries beneath the ground. All at once they had become secret; they had been buried along roads; they had been excommunicated from all the colonial pulpits; they had been persecuted like their creators by centurions and butchers. But from under the earth or from under the water, after those centuries of darkness, they continue to reappear, continue to afford an everlasting testimony to an undying, multifaceted greatness.

In my *Canto Generale,* I narrated how the conquistador Pizarro dragged the Inca king in chains into a room in one of the palaces of his kingdom, announcing that in a few weeks' time he, Pizarro, would have him executed. They were going to cut his throat like a lamb at a sacrifice, like a slave earmarked for martyrdom — there in the main courtyard of his own palace, in front of all his princes, his chiefs, his priests, his womenfolk, his children, and his musicians. This, at least, was what was going to come to pass, the conquistador told him, if his subjects failed to bring in, from each and every province, however remote, all the gold of Peru. "But how much gold, how much?" asked the Inca, his innocent eyes meeting those of his captor. And Pizarro replied: "Lift your hand as high as you can and draw a line as blue as your own blood around this room. Then order your vassals to fill the room with gold up to the line your hand has drawn."

For minutes, hours, and weeks that dragged on like centuries, messengers, priests, princes, musicians, humiliated warriors, stunned peasants, and desperate women ran and trotted, flew like bees, and scurried up and down the empire with amphoras of gold, with statues, vases, bracelets, necklaces, utensils, thrones, and sculptures of the precious metal. At last the ransom brought in as a result of all this agonizing went beyond the line traced out by the hand of the Inca.

In the end, all this gold proved worthless to the Inca king, for Pizarro had him garroted to death. But many of the couriers and messengers bearing gold, and who had placed their faith in the words of the butcher, heard the terrible news on the shores of a lake while they were sleeping, each one with a sack of gold at his side. And then, filled with terror by the news of the Great Death, they cursed and wept and buried forever the treasures that would never arrive at the royal palace in time to rise above the blue line traced by the executed emperor.

The sublime essence of Latin America revealed itself to me in the form of its aerial edifice at the proud, solitary citadel of Machu Picchu. It was one of the decisive encounters of my life, occurring around the year 1943. The great war then being fought by the Europeans gave no sign of drawing to a conclusion. Goya had prophesied: "The sleep of reason generates monsters." While reason was asleep in the world, the monsters indulged in supreme butchery. Since the time of sufferings of pre-Columbian America — when, according to Father Las Casas, the dogs of invaders were often fed the flesh of living prisoners, men, women, and children — reason had never had such a tragic slumber. Degradation, martyrdom, and annihilation were put into practice methodically. The deafening thunder of shelling and bombing came to us from ancient, classical Europe, and from remote countries we followed a trail of blood that led us through the night and across the seas to the onetime scene of culture, which had now been transformed in subjection and agony.

I happened to be returning from Mexico, full of the pain all this caused me, and although I was not altogether losing my indestructible faith in the persistence of human goodness, I was disoriented and drained of energy by that turn suddenly taken by our dark era. On the back of mules we climbed up steep, rugged trails to the once-lost and now-remembered city, the mystery-shrouded Machu Picchu. That lofty city had been ashamed of its own time, had fallen silent and hidden itself in its forest. What had become of its builders, its inhabitants? What had they left behind, aside from the dignity of stone, to tell us of their lives, their hopes and aims, their disappearance? A deep, resounding silence was the only reply.

I was already familiar with the silence of other monumental ruins, but it had always been a humiliated silence, the silence of marbles defeated once and for all. There in the heights of Peru, on the other hand, this majestic architecture had preserved itself secretly in the silence of the Andean peaks. The sacred ruins were surrounded on every side by the sky. The green forest was mottled here and there by small, swiftly flying clouds that passed lightly overhead, kissing that splendid product of the eternal essence in man. Looming up at the highest point in the city was the *intihuatana,* or "sundial," a sort of calendar of immense stones, with a verticil perhaps destined to mark the passing of hours in those extreme heights. These astronomical dials were tenaciously wiped out by the conquistadors, doggedly determined as ever to destroy the nucleus of culture. But the city of Machu Picchu defeated them; it hid itself under its own creepers, it multiplied its mantle of green, and the destructive intruders passed by without even suspecting its existence.

Machu Picchu revealed itself to me as the survival of reason in the face of delirium. The absence of its creators, the mystery of its origin and of its mute tenacity were an object lesson on the order that man, with his firm resolve, can bring into being down through the centuries. It is a collective building effort capable of challenging the disorder of nature and human misfortune alike. I recalled the edifices of Teotihuacán, the buildings of Monte Alban, Chichén-Itzá, the temples of Palenque, the religious pyramids of prodigious proportions and radiant symmetry, which climbed toward blood and light throughout the entire Mexican territory. It became clear to me that above and beyond the structures lost in martyrdom and darkness, above and beyond the infinite formal creation of figures, jewels, and subterranean objects, above and beyond the defeated immensity of that America that continues germinating day after day from its own dark roots, the ancient American masters had erected an aerial, invulnerable soul capable of challenging with its own being both foreign domination and the dogged waves of aggression and forgetfulness. These discoveries opened up many roads to me, including that of the harmony between my own destiny and that time-defeating truth, those collective creations in which all the component parts — hope and suffering, delicacy and power — were joined over and over again into one central organism that directed all possibilities of action and spawned a new, sonorous silence, fraught with intelligence and the sound of music.

One must add to this wealth the monuments of buried poetry, the Aztec and Tlaxcalan odes in honor of kings and princes, festive odes and ritual odes, the ancient poetry of the extreme south, of Andean Peruvians and Aymaras, a poetry of the sweetest melancholy, like the murmuring of water through foliage, through the passing of the time that has brought down races. A Mayan text like *Popol-Vuh,* for instance, is a miracle, an enchanting "Book of Genesis" that explains and narrates the beginnings of human life, customs, and rites with the sureness of an eyewitness. In its pages it is not easy to separate the substance of dreams and idolatry, of real events, of prophecy. It is a fundamental monument of man in any course he might steer. It is a monument of religion and irreligion: a brief hymn to the growth and unfolding of life on earth. (And yet we know that a priest, the Archbishop of Yucatan, was among those who saw to the destruction of thousands of Mayan manuscripts accumulated down through the centuries.)

What is the relationship, a few, perhaps many, will ask, between the new and ancient American cultures? I admit that the colonial condition imposed on our Latin America represents not only an obstinate domination but also a disruption of incalculable proportions. The old mold was violated and broken to bits. The relationships became clandestine, they grew weak for terror, they spread out to remote villages, and in the end became extinct. It was only in some small marketplace or fair that the vases, toys, or few poor fabrics once again put in an appearance. As to sculpture, architecture, poetry, narrative, and dancing — all this was swallowed up by the earth. It lay down with the colony to sleep a sleep from which there has still been no awakening.

A few far-off echoes of the prodigious tradition appeared in the Mexican school of painting, in Orozco, Siqueiros, Rivera, and Tamayo. But in all these creators' efforts, one perceives a reproductive reflection, an intellectual expressionism in the place of the primeval freshness of the ancient, long-sealed-off sources. Lam and Matta have at the same time sought to a certain extent to reach out toward the lost continuity, but

9

their major works, although they aim at terror and enigma, fail to generate true fear in us or to pose questions like the ancient profound works of pre-Columbian America. Some Europeans, such as Henry Moore, and some sculptors, such as Penalba and Colvin, Americans by birth, also seek to breathe new life into our tremendous legacy. But it was the Brazilian scholar and architect, Oscar Niemeyer, with his grandiose Brasilia, a collective and time-defying rose, who came closest to the spacious, airy architecture of the ancient Americans.

In the field of poetry, Latin American versifiers, with a few praiseworthy exceptions, have fled in horror from our own cosmic density, and have not even taken as models Jorge Manrique, Soto de Rojas, or Quevedo, but *Monsieur* Péret or *Monsieur* Artaud. The Latin-American novel, however, with García Márquez and other outstanding protagonists of our time, has taken a great leap, continuing the communication that had been rent asunder. It is only a first harbinger of an insurrection or a resurrection of a possible greatness.

I know not why my words always take the form of a voyage, although perhaps the voyage is only one toward the past or toward silence. It comes to me that we have done nothing more than scratch the surface, and perhaps only at the edges, of a soul-stirring, multifarious culture. All I wished to do was to stroll along the remote roads that the native American populated down through the centuries with extraordinary creations, forgotten myths, and battles that ended in defeat. But not even tireless scholars and titanic researchers will ever be able to provide us with a catalog or a key to the immense treasure that has been left behind. Their interpretations will forever remain only halfway to the truth. Nor can detailed photographs taken from only a few feet away or from the most modern helicopters ever fully reveal to us that burning miracle itself or its illusive legacy to us. The museums of the entire world show us only a few memorials of one of the greatest adventures in the creative power of man, that which took shape in the far-flung regions of the American planet. The analysis, study, and illumination of these infinite works will always remain a fundamental challenge to science.

But I myself, a creature of these very latitudes, dare not catalog, denominate, or assert. I shall continue throughout the days or years of my life to nurture the admiration, terror, and tenderness with which all these prodigious works have marked my existence. And I shall continue to feel myself minimal, non-existent before the greatness of that splendor. May the American land one day be worthy of the richly varied monuments handed down to us by these peoples who have faded from our view.

Pablo Neruda

INTRODUCTION

Situated in the vast stretch of land descending from the heights of the Andes westward down to the Pacific Ocean are the remains of one of the more enigmatic civilizations that mankind has produced. Even to this day, centuries after this civilization was obliterated, its material remains may be seen in Colombia, through much of Ecuador, throughout Peru, in the Bolivian highlands, in Chile, and even into a section of Argentina. This territory, as large as Italy, France, and Spain combined, quite naturally divides into three irregular vertical strips: the seacoast, the highlands, and the tropical forest. This subdivision, which Peruvian schoolchildren repeat by rote from their first lessons in geography, had a considerable influence on Andean history and civilization.

The three strips run from north to south, but the mountains that run down through the center are broken by a series of intermontane valleys and several large upland basins, and these have inevitably served as the focal points for human habitation. Meanwhile, the numerous streams and rivers, their sources hidden in the snowcapped peaks of high plateaus of the Andes, rarely succeed in piercing the western bastion to flow into the Pacific. Instead, they head for the forests to the east and many of them eventually join and swell to form the world's largest river, the Amazon.

In the central highlands, north of Cuzco — where the "navel of the world" was sited by the Inca — the Ucayali River is formed from the Urubamba and the Apurimac. Beginning amid the eternal snows of the Andean peaks, these rivers flow — and often plunge headlong — down the mountain slopes to the west, irrigating the bare, desolate territories of the plateaus, and later seeking a ravine or canyon to make their way down through the luxuriant vegetation of the Amazonian jungle.

This jungle marks the eastern boundary of the Andean territory, a boundary that — judging by the fact that it is still largely unexplored — appears to be more impassable than the Pacific Ocean. The last Inca before the Spanish conquest must have been fully aware that those rivers flowing eastward through their territory had to empty somewhere into another ocean. Nevertheless, the jungle remained between them and the unknown like some great green curtain drawn by the hand of an invincible nature. There is still no proof that the natives ever attempted to navigate the Marañon, the river in the northern sector of the highlands that joins with the Ucayali to form the Amazon. Yet the ancient Peruvians seem to have navigated the Pacific, at least to the nearest islands and possibly even to the distant Polynesian archipelago.

If the high plateaus were the seed ground of the Andean cultures, the coast was perhaps their nursery: it was on the coast that the first known communities of fishermen and farmers came into being. This is easily enough explained. The coast is made up of a narrow strip of rugged, often desolate country, furrowed by short rivers that spring from the western slopes of the Andes and drain into the Pacific, thus forming small fertile valleys divided by mountains or sand deserts. This is the case, at least, south of the Gulf of Guayaquil — in other words, along virtually the entire coast of the Peru of today. And this was the richest area, culturally speaking, of the pre-Inca world, when the Classical Period of the Mochica and Nazca cultures flourished, for instance, to be followed by that of the Chimú culture.

North of Guayaquil, however — that is to say, all along the coast of Ecuador and of the ancient kingdom of Quito — the central zone is strongly influenced by the equatorial climatic conditions. This northern coast is humid and luxuriant, and the valleys along the various rivers were inhabited by populations that still lived in primitive communities when the Spanish landed at Tumbez Bay in 1532 to begin their conquest of the Andes.

The difference in climate and vegetation between the southern and northern coasts in the ancient territory of the Inca results primarily from the marine currents. A great body of cold water flows out of the Pacific and eastward toward South America; after it runs against the Chilean coast, this current heads north and, near the mouth of the Piura River, it meets the *El Niño,* a countercurrent with warmer, deep-blue waters from the tropics that pushes the cold current farther out to sea and forces it to veer northwest. The cold current, of course, is the Humboldt Current, so named after the nineteenth-century German geographer who discovered and studied it; he explained that its cold waters came from the Antarctic, but it is now thought that at least some of the cold water wells up from the deep trough along the coast of South America.

Whatever its source, the Humboldt Current has a temperature averaging about 5°F. colder than other waters of the same latitude and the air above it. It even takes on a greenish color as it cuts into the blue waters of the Pacific. But quite aside from the natural phenomenon, the Humboldt Current is important for the influence it has exerted on the coastal cultures of South America. The relatively low and constant temperature of the waters is accompanied by a lesser degree of salinity, and this facilitates the growth of plankton; the presence of this food source attracts large quantities of fish; these convert the green ribbon of the Humboldt Current into a favorite hunting ground for myriads of sea birds; and these birds drop their excrement along the coast to form veritable mountains of guano, the natural nitrogenous fertilizer that to this day represents one of this coast's chief sources of wealth. This is why the Peruvian coast, south of the mouth of the Piura River (which issues into an inlet of the great promontory forming the Gulf of Guayaquil on the north) remains so dry and desertlike. The Andes Mountains form a natural barrier against the clouds drifting from the east, while the Humboldt Current, due to its cooler temperature, drains the breezes off in the sea. Rain, known locally as *garrua,* is so rare along the Peruvian coast that it is usually little more than a drizzle; and when that pattern is periodically broken, the rain ends by destroying the harvests and all buildings made of mud and unbaked bricks.

So it is that little of the early coastal cultures has remained for the archaeologists except for certain extraordinary monuments and what materials have been found in graves. It was on the high plateaus of the Andes that the later civilization of the Inca arose, as well as several of their predecessors, and it was a civilization dominated by stone. And stone was ever-present like a god — an irascible god, too, for earthquakes brought such upheavals to this land as to remold the profiles of the landscape. According to some recent archaeological theories, the civilization of the Andes ruled the ancient coastal peoples for some two centuries before the Spanish conquest, precisely because they, the mountain people, were "harder" — ruder and more authoritarian. But however fascinating such theories may be, there is little tangible evidence to support them.

In this connection, we should recall the celebrated questioning of the *quipucamayocs,* the court record-keepers of the Inca king, Atahualpa, by the Spanish Viceroy, Francisco de Toledo. This questioning was so biased and those interrogated were so badly frightened throughout as to leave the researcher of today with very little that can be considered believable. Meanwhile, the Indian Filipillo, the interpreter of Pizarro, is remembered as one of the most faithless translators of Andean history, a schemer who was always seeking to edit in his own favor the talks between the Spaniards and the natives. And if the King of Spain received a "black legend" and a "rose-colored" one from America regarding the native peoples, we must realize how much self-interest motivated the correspondents. The Conquistadors painted the American Indian in dark colors to obtain more supplies and greater recognition for their exploits; the missionaries did everything in their power to demonstrate that the Indians were meek and ready not for the sword but for the Gospel.

This is one of the reasons the Inca world has remained something of an enigma up to our own time. There has had to be considerable guesswork — some intelligent, some successful — in directing any rays of light onto this or that group of ruins or this or that moment in history. Of course, there are the fascinating accounts set down by such early chroniclers as Garcilaso de la Vega and others, but as we shall discuss later, they are hardly to be accepted as altogether reliable. (On page 187 may be found some notes on the several early sources quoted most extensively in this volume, both in the main text and in the marginal "anthology.")

But, in general, we shall avoid becoming involved in the critical and interpretive considerations of the "historical" sources. Instead, we shall be drawing more on the work of modern, disciplined archaeologists in attempting to supply a logical key to the various Andean monuments from the standpoint of architectural elements and the development of an urban culture. In particular, we shall emphasize the concept that architecture must inevitably fit in with the surroundings and the social needs of a civilization with the characteristics of that which arose in the Andes. And above all, before we can hope to understand the climax civilization of the Inca — whether their monuments or their society — we must look closely at the deep roots of both in the earlier cultures of the Andes.

Two rather specific problems might be mentioned here, simply to dispose of them once and for all in this volume. One is the use of the word "Inca." Originally it referred to a relatively restricted group of related families who led the dynastic rise and the imperial expansion that centered on Cuzco; once in control, they themselves extended the term to refer to all speakers of their language. The Spanish came along and confused things by extending the word to all subjects of the vast Inca-dominated empire, and also by narrowing "the Inca" to refer to the emperor himself. To simplify matters, our text uses the term essentially in its original sense and then, by an extension of this, to refer to all the people, forces, and elements identified with the operation of the empire, whose ruler we shall call "the emperor." (And by general usage, "Inca" is both the singular and plural form.)

Meanwhile, the problem of chronology is less easily resolved. We have provided a chronological chart (p. 182), and throughout the text we must continually assign dates and lengths of time to periods, names to periods and cultures, and sites and artifacts to periods. In a work of this kind, we cannot become involved in the detailed discussions that attend such matters in the specialists' literature. What we can do is to warn readers that all these matters are rather fluid and controversial, with few authorities agreeing on all the details. Having acknowledged that, we have then proceeded to settle here and there on personal judgments, but always within the reasonable parameters set by most authorities.

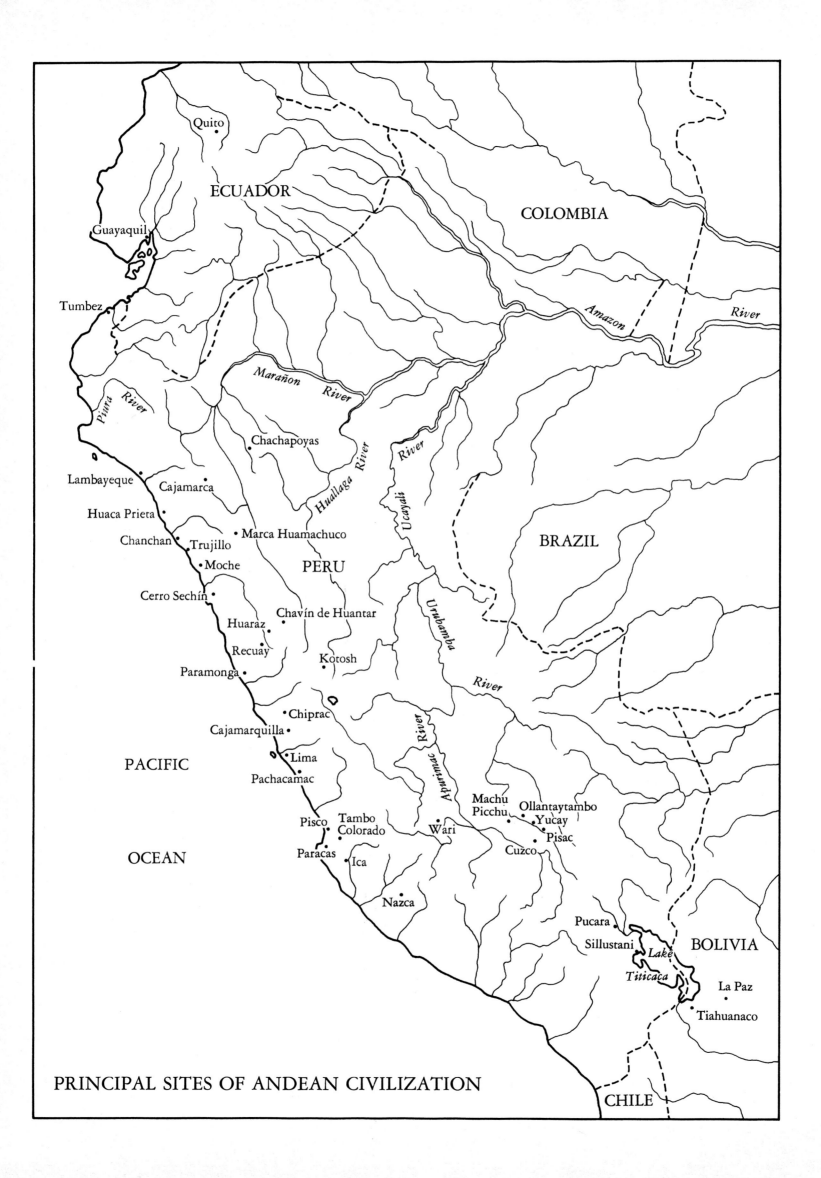

PRINCIPAL SITES OF ANDEAN CIVILIZATION

EARLY ANDEAN CULTURES

Early Man in the Andes

Ever since the Spanish carried back the first reports of the exotic inhabitants of the New World, people have speculated on the origins of the American Indians. At first the problem was to relate them to the Biblical accounts of human origins; eventually this approach faded. But since the sixteenth century, explorers, naturalists, scholars, and others — more or less learned, as the case may be — have attempted to establish that the first inhabitants of the Americas came from such places as Egypt or wherever the "root stocks" or "originators of civilization" are thought to have lived. As for the Andean populations who are to concern us, there have been various specific efforts to pinpoint their origins. Not too long ago, while one group of intrepid men were floating from Africa to America on a raft to prove that the bearers of civilization came from that direction, another group were floating on a raft from the Pacific to prove that the South American Indians came from that direction. There have also been attempts to make much of certain linguistic affinities between the inhabitants of the Andes and those of Polynesia and Easter Island.

Now there may well have been some contact between the early peoples of the Andes and those living around the Pacific Ocean. Indeed, a reputable group of scholars can point to a significant mass of evidence that seems to suggest that there were at least random individuals or groups from Asia (Japan, India, Southeast Asia, etc.) who introduced certain cultural artifacts and processes to the American Indians. But this was thousands of years after the Indians were well settled there, and has nothing to do with the origins of the people or, for that matter, of the basic cultural fabric.

The fact is, it is now generally accepted by all authorities that the ancestors of the Indians of South America — as of those of Middle and North America — came from Asia across the Bering Strait region and spread through the Americas, moving ever farther afield and ever southward in search of new food sources and living space. The real question is when this took place. Again, it is generally agreed that there were early representatives of these first Americans living near the very tip of South America as early as 8000–9000 B.C. The first people in the Central Andes — the region centering on Peru — must have arrived well before that, at least by 10,000 B.C. These dates, by the way, are not mere speculation: they are based on bones of humans and animals dated by radioactive carbon. Still, it must be understood that this chronology is open-ended, and it is likely to change as new discoveries are made.

It is assumed that the point of entry and the main route into South America was across the Colombian Andes and then southward down the Andes; evidence of these first "Andeans," however, is scarce as they were hunters and food-gatherers who lacked almost all forms of material culture; but a few cave and rock shelter sites have been explored, and various stone tools and weapons have been found. Relatively early — at least by 7,000 B.C. — some of the migrants made their way down the western slopes of the Andes to the Pacific and began to exploit the natural resources of the coastal plains with their swampy lagoons and fertile meadows; there were plenty of birds and small game to kill and a variety of wild plants to eat.

It was not until about 4000 B.C., though, that the next development occurred. The first people along the coast had not paid much attention to the sea, nor had they really settled down. But small villages, settlements at least, began to develop near the mouths of the rivers that drain the western slopes of the Andes along the Pacific coast of Peru; these sites are in the Chicama Valley, the Viru Valley, near Pacasmayo, in the valleys of the

Chavín Art: The formal abstraction and the curvilinear decorative seals of this monochrome vase are typical of the Chavín style.

Paracas, Chilloa, and Nazca, and elsewhere. And these people were exploiting the sea — attested by the large middens, or refuse mounds, with their centuries of accumulated shellfish and bones of fishes and sea-lions, gourds used as net floats, even fragments of nets themselves. Although occasionally they killed deer or birds or some other wild game, these people seem to have essentially stopped hunting.

But meanwhile they turned to something else: they began simple farming. Perhaps the fullest picture of life at one of these settlements has emerged from Huaca Prieta ("dark mound") in the Chicama Valley on the northern coast of Peru. It was a mound about forty-five feet high, made up of the remains of food, tools, and other artifacts of the villagers who inhabited the site continuously from about 2500 to 1200 B.C. Hunting weapons and bones of land animals are not found here, but there are vast quantities of remains of sea life, as well as the many gourds used for net floats. They gathered some wild plants, but they were also cultivating some — squash, gourds, beans, chile pepper, and certain roots and tubers. These people never did have pottery; they used gourds as vessels, and did much of their cooking with hot stones.

From the many remnants of fabrics, bags, and fishing nets, however, it is clear that these people grew and spun cotton (as well as a bast fiber made from a species of milkweed). The fabrics were made by hand, mostly by twining, but they could perform simple weaving and they produced simple designs by manipulation of the warp. What was missing from the Huaca Prieta mound, however, was maize, which had been cultivated in Middle America for many hundreds of years. It is believed that it was introduced into Peru as early as 1400 B.C. from Mexico, but it

Chavín de Huantar: These drawings of stone bas-reliefs reveal zoomorphic monsters of particular technical achievement. The upper one represents a condor, the lower one a puma with a snake over it.

Chavín de Huantar: A bas-relief with a feline
figure probably inspired by a puma.

was to be several centuries before it took on any significance in the diet or life of the Andean Indians.

What dwellings there were at Huaca Prieta belonged to the settlement's latest period; the structures were mostly oval-shaped and were half underground; the interiors were lined with stones, while the roofs were of stone or clay and supported by crossbeams or whalebones. Such archaic dwellings appear to have been standard along the Peruvian coast, although as with many of the elements of this period, there were minor local variants. In the Viru Valley to the north, for instance, there were buildings made entirely of clay. Abandoned underground houses, incidentally, were sometimes used as tombs.

Although the settlements shared many common characteristics, the peoples populating the Peruvian coast formed what the French ethnologist Louis Baudin has called "a human archipelago." Each settlement tended to be little more than a group of crude dwellings around a clearing, with the cultivated fields crowding close around them; there might be a number of such settlements strewn out along a river valley, but between one valley and another there were hundreds of miles of mountains or deserts. The great distances, the lack of pack animals, the earthquakes, the rugged terrain, all came to determine the strictly sedentary nature of the primitive populations as well as the persistent traditions of the various Andean cultures that were to follow.

We have just said that there were no pack animals, and in the early stage of Andean culture there were none. The only domesticated animal these early farmers had was the small indigenous dog; later they would keep the cavy, or guinea pig, as a source of meat. But the early Andeans also hunted the llama and its various relatives — the guanaco, the alpacas, and the vicuña — which lived in the highlands. Eventually they maintained large herds of llamas and alpacas in the highlands; the alpacas were prized mainly for their fine wool, but the llama provided meat, a coarse wool, and fertilizer. And somewhere along the way, the Andeans domesticated the llama as a pack animal — although it will not budge with much more than 100 pounds. All these four "cousins," by the way, are in turn relatives of the camel, which the early Spanish recognized by calling the llama "the little American camel."

Little can be known for certain of the religious or social life of these early Andeans. The systematic and brutal destruction by the Spanish of all external signs of cults practiced prior to the Conquest has obliterated whatever might have survived into the time of the Inca. But certain things may be inferred — from what few surviving elements there are — from certain projections backward from the Inca times, and from our general knowledge of early religious and social life. It is assumed, for instance, that the religion of the early farmers was bound up with the worship of their ancestors. There were a few goods buried in the graves at Huaca Prieta, just enough to suggest that they already believed that the dead would want some things for a kind of afterlife.

Up until recently, at least, there was a tendency among students of the Andean Indians to endow any structure with the significance of a temple, any pile of stones with that of a totem. We must be cautious about making such emphatic projections of the later Inca religion back on to these people. But from all we know, it seems safe to say that the religious spirit of the early Andeans was essentially pantheistic, inspired by animals such as the puma, the falcon, or the condor, but also strongly linked to objects, particularly unusual ones such as an oddly shaped stone or a root. (Even as late as Inca times — as was pointed out to Father Francisco de Avila, who interrogated the native Andeans in 1620 — a person with some physical anomaly might be raised to the rank of village "protector." (A fuller impression of the Andean Indians' religion is provided in the Appendix, pages 178–81.)

If we were to seek a symbol of this early Andean culture, one that would prefigure the many phases yet to come, it would be in the failure of the Andeans to invent the wheel. (The Middle Americans seem to have known of the wheel for toys or ritual objects.) They never used the wheel for transport, nor for any of the tools to be derived from it, such as the

Chavín de Huantar: Drawings of bas-reliefs with typical anthropomorphic and zoomorphic images.

Chavín de Huantar: On the two stone slabs above, the one on the left has a variant of the monster-figure with hair of snakes, while the one on the right has abstract stylized motifs.

Following pages:
Chavín de Huantar: This close-up of the outer wall of the Castillo reveals the regular alternation of the rows of stones of different thicknesses.

lathe and the winch — not even the potter's wheel. Similarly, although abundant deposits of iron were to be found in their territory, the Andean Indians never discovered iron. Both the achievements and the limitations of the Andeans to come should be viewed in the light of this deep-rooted and archaic traditionalism. It helps us to remember, for instance, that for masses of Andean Indians in the centuries to follow, the basic texture of their daily life would hardly change.

The Formative Period

The appearance of pottery at Peruvian sites about 1200 B.C. becomes the signal for a whole sequence of development, a virtual flowering of Andean culture that is known as the "Formative Period." This, in turn, is conventionally divided into two parts. One — from about 1200 to 300 B.C. — is known as the "cultist period," so named because it is characterized by the spread of religious activity. The second part is often called the "experimenter period," but we shall emphasize a different aspect by calling it the "regional–state period": running from about 300 B.C. to A.D. 200, it saw the formation of territorial units that were to develop into the complex state organisms of the classical and post-classical stages.

The invention of pottery is usually taken as one of the major thresholds of a developing culture; when it appears in the Andes, it is already so well made and varied that it seems likely that it was introduced from Middle America. In any case, it was still some time before pots were used for cooking. There were other developments in craftsmanship, too — in textiles, tools, metalwork (gold), etc. Although people still fished, hunted, and gathered foods, they now seem to have subsisted principally on cultivated crops. With this more settled agricultural life, villages began to develop; and with a more concentrated village life, religious activity also became more intense.

The relationship among community, subsistence patterns, religion, and state was inherent in Andean life from an early stage. The Indians erected *huacas,* for instance, a monument marking or symbolizing the tomb of an often legendary ancestor or founder of a family or community inhabiting a settlement. The *huaca* — originally a mere pile of stones — was usually erected in the center of the settlement and was cared for by the entire community. As contacts with nearby settlements increased, the people tended to abandon their endogamous — and probably matrilineal — phase. This led to the fusion of different customs, and also of different *huacas* into true villages; and where the desire was present, these villages could find a mythical ancestor in common, an ancestor who became the guardian divinity of the village, replacing the ancient *huacas.*

The basic Andean community unit is called to this day — in the Quechua language, the descendant of the Inca language — the *ayllu,* and it probably goes back to this original *huaca* orientation and the common ownership of land. The *ayllu* remained a group of extended families, both in the sense that the members considered themselves descendants of a common ancestor — and were in fact literally closely related — and in the sense that their survival depended on their communal economic-productive activities. Possibly one of the major factors in the new communal sense of the cultist period was the cultivation of maize, which by about 900 B.C. was becoming an important part of the Andean diet, so much so that it was also becoming part of their broader concerns. Maize represented fertility and community: if people were willing to cooperate in clearing and cultivating their fields of maize — and assuming the gods were kind when it came to the proper weather conditions — they could grow the basic food for a relatively small percentage of a year's daily labor. Maize thus became a symbol of patience and stability. Along with this cooperative-organized labor came increased leisure, some of which time could be given over to building structures for the burgeoning religious activities.

The common village buildings and the dwellings of the masses in the residential quarters — frequently of considerable dimensions — were still made of perishable materials, wood, *adobe,* mud-and-straw. But with

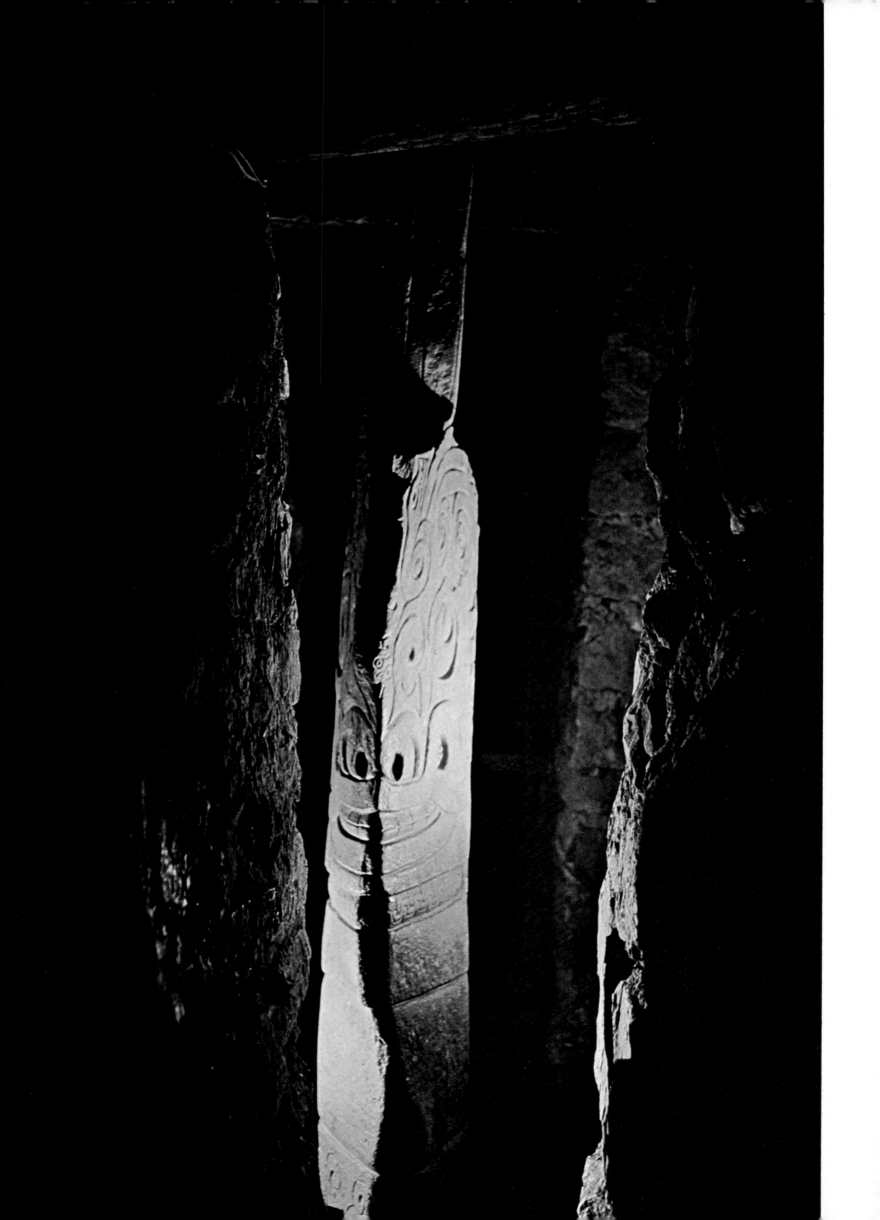

Above:
Chavín de Huantar: At the Castillo, the fallen fragments of a stone frieze reveal the flock of condors (one of which is shown in the drawing on page 18).

Left:
Chavín de Huantar: The frontal view of the *Lanzón* at the intersection of two of the main galleries within the Castillo. The granite monolith, fifteen feet high, is solidly embedded in the stone of the floor and the ceiling.

A

B

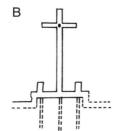

C

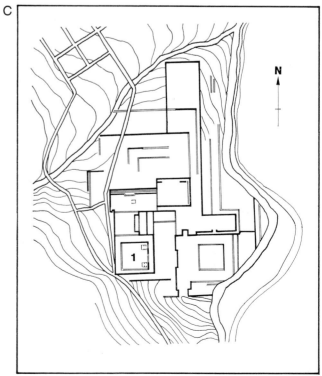

Right:
A) *This drawing of the profile of the* Lanzón *head clearly reveals the fangs and the snake hair.*
B) *The plan of a section of the galleries in the Castillo indicates (with the dot) the position of the* Lanzón.
C) *A plan of the archaeological zone of Chavín de Huantar shows (1) the position of the Castillo.*

the concentration of economic resources of larger territorial areas, "sanctuaries" began to develop, often with imposing buildings in which the use of stone, architectural sculpture, and advanced building techniques were placed at the service of essentially religious-ceremonial functions.

Eventually, the *ayllus,* or village units, began to maintain more direct contacts with one another — more, that is, than occasional meetings at religious centers. This gave rise to the groupings of villages based on the theocratic system that had developed along with the cults and the sanctuaries; with this we arrive at the "regional-state" development of the Formative Period. Among the other concomitants of such federations was the pooling of labor in the interests of the entire community — projects such as irrigation works, bridges, terracing.

Chavín de Huantar

The cultist period, of course, had many local cultural variants, but it was marked by a certain pervading style, what is known by archaeologists as a "horizon": a single distinguishing element or a conglomerate of several elements that characterize a period throughout a wide geographical area. The cultist period is recognized by the Chavín Horizon, the most evident characteristic of which is the highly stylized feline design, a catlike image — based on the puma or jaguar — that recurs in carvings, stone sculpture, bonework, metal work, pottery, and textiles.

The determinant role as a center for the elaboration and long-range exportation of this first important Andean cultural style is ascribed to the site of Chavín de Huantar, located in the upper valley of the Marañon River, where it crosses the northern Andean area of Peru. The extent of its influence, in an area that also includes much of the coast, enables us to consider the Chavín style as one of the models on which the coastal states of the classical period were to build centuries later.

The exceptional development of Chavín de Huantar, situated in a narrow, easily defensible valley, was primarily due to its ideal position for the filtering of traffic between the northern Andes and the southern territories, and between the coast and the regions to the east. This was the route followed by the main Andean "crest" road, in fact, and looming in this hinge area was the great sanctuary of Chavín. There are many buildings spread over a large area here, but the basic units are arranged around a large sunken court; few of the remains indicate that this great complex was used as a residential community. The most impressive structure, which lies somewhat apart from the central court, is the Castillo, so named by the early Spanish discoverers. It probably served as a combination fortress-castle, a religious sanctuary, a supply storehouse, and a landmark.

The Castillo is a massive edifice, 245 feet square at its base and 43 feet at its highest point; it is composed of two main terraces, or platforms, of granite cemented with clay. The exterior wall is made up of horizontal rows of well-dressed stones, frequently in an alternating form of one row of thick stones and two rows of thin ones. Tenoned into the lower part of the wall were carved heads, human in shape but many with feline tusks: this is the first appearance of an architectural element that will recur frequently throughout pre-Inca Peru. Running around the upper part of the wall was a cornice, or a sort of frieze, once adorned with finely incised stone slabs; these have all fallen and have disappeared from the site.

The interior of the Castillo had three floors; ramps and stairs connected the floors, and there was a system of ventilating shafts. Each floor had a complicated series of rooms and galleries lined with stone; the galleries were about six feet high and 40 inches wide. Solidly fixed in the pavement and stone ceiling at the intersection of the Castillo's main galleries is a granite monolith in the shape of a prism — somewhat like a spear with the point turned down: it is known, in fact, as the *Lanzón* ("spearhead"). About 15 feet high, this stone is decorated with bas-reliefs of the head of a monster and other motifs. (See page 24.)

The head evidently represents a divinity with a range of characteristics. It has the smirking mouth typical of the Chavín style, with two lateral

Chavín de Huantar: One of the stone heads embedded in the outer wall of the Castillo represents a typical monster with fangs.

Following pages:
Kotosh: This picture shows the archaeological excavation in progress at this relatively recently discovered site, not far from Chavín de Huantar.

fangs and the hair of serpents; it can be assigned to that category of polymorphous divinities formed from a number of different zoomorphic patterns but in which the feline and serpentine elements seem dominant. But the importance of the *Lanzón* undoubtedly lies more in its unusual situation in this significant structure than in the literal significance of the sacred figure carved on its surface. We find ourselves confronting an example — one of the earliest — of the integration of a work of sculpture with an architectural space. As such, it merits further speculations, for it may provide a key to the interpretation of the monuments of the later Andean civilizations as well as to its meaning for the Chavín people.

The mystery of the *Lanzón* may perhaps best be approached from the viewpoint of the magical-religious interpretation of the fundamental relationships between the various physical elements of nature and human civilization. Thus, it has been driven into the ground like the golden staff that Manco Capac, the mythical forefather of the Inca, was to see swallowed by the earth at the place where the first sanctuary of the sun and, later, the sacred city of Cuzco, were to be founded. In this sense, it marks the vertical for the exact localization of the "navel" of the territory and society of Chavín; in this interpretation, we must keep in mind that the successive pre-Inca and Inca uses of the concept of "navel of the world" extended to the entire area belonging to the politico-religious organization, not just to the sanctuary site.

It seems obvious, too, that the carved idol-head aims at producing the sensation of a miraculous penetration of the *Lanzón* into the rock without the intervention of human beings. This idol, then, becomes the "demon" of the locality. But beyond that, it is the symbol of the organization of all external space around one vertical axis. The mystery of the unity of space, hidden in the apparent monstrousness of the god, is clearly hinted at by the position of the sculpture at the intersection of the four galleries. These are the four "main roads," the four geographical directions, the four cardinal points, and (in accordance with a belief widely held in pre-Columbian America) the "four cables" holding up the four quarters of the world. The secret enclosed in the central point — the idol — since it comes from the divinity and is in perennial contact with both the terrestrial and celestial worlds, is thereby unraveled: it is the first clear reference to the world as made up of the structures of man.

The *Lanzón,* on guard at the crossroads of the two fundamental axes of the cosmos, and in the most sacred and secret part of the Castillo — itself, remember, situated at the crossroads of the Andes for these people — anticipates the development of Inca cosmology. Centuries later the elements symbolized in this monolith were to provide the basis for the state organization and administrative systems of the Inca Empire centered at Cuzco. Passing through various intermediary stages — whose essential aspects we shall consider as we move along — the "spatial mysticism" emerged by stages from the most obscure and remote origins in the pre-Chavín culture, engendering as its chief result a typical Andean way of conceiving the unity of the state in terms of sacred geometry, while preserving the religious mystery for the service of a closed, elect caste.

The "multiform monster" of the *Lanzón* thus reveals itself to be space itself, which from a single central seed germinates the infinite multiplications and ramifications useful in mirroring and organizing in a rational fashion the religious beliefs and the very structure of society. It was, in fact, around a sacred stone or pile of stones (the *huaca*) that the first small agricultural communities united; then the sanctuary-centers, the city-states, and finally the great regional-states came to be organized around ever-more ambitious sacred stones.

Incidentally, the *Lanzón* is not the only image at Chavín that can be interpreted as the monster symbolizing the totality of space, the "one sole multiform being." We may interpret in this sense the Raimondi Stele (named after its discoverer in 1873), which was located on the exterior "crown" of the Castillo. It is a large slab of diorite, about 6½ feet high, and according to recent interpretations the stele represents the monstrous figure of the zoomorphic mask so widespread in later Nazca pottery. Like the *Lanzón,* the stele carvings are rendered with rigorous sym-

Left:
Kotosh: A view of the "temple of crossed hands."

Right:
Kotosh: A close-up of the bas-relief of the "crossed hands" that gave the temple its current name; the clay relief is under one of the niches in the main wall.

Below:
Kotosh: A view of the inner side of the main wall, facing north, of the "crossed-hands temple."

Left:
Cerro Sechín: Two adjacent stone carvings, the one on the left representing a warrior, the one on the right comprising three heads piled on top of each other.

HYMN TO THE RAIN

Lovely princess,
thy brother
hath just shattered
thy urn,
and this is why
the thunder grumbles,
the lightning flashes,
the thunderbolts strike.
But thou art the one, princess,
who must give us water,
making it rain
and snow and hail.
The Creator of the World,
Pachacamac Viracocha,
created thee
for this task.

GARCILASO DE LA VEGA: *Comentarios Reales* (1609)

HUANCAN LOVE SONG

Amid rags I sleep,
my lot is poverty.
Because of thee I shall leave this place.
I sleep, this is how I sleep,
thy net snares and joins.
Rain, thou bearer of water,
oh Chunaychunay, heart fraternal,
part of the great festivity
that leaves and never returns.
Injure me not, little brother,
for on that day my heart wept.

POMA DE AYALA: *Nueva corónica* (1613)

RELIGIOUS POEM

Of the world above
and the one below
as of the immense ocean,
the Creator.
Of the conqueror of all things,
of all that seethes and boils,
be it man or woman,
so saying, ordaining
of the true woman,
I fashioned thee.
Who art thou?
Where?
And what does thou think?
Oh speak, speak!

JUAN DE SANTA CRUZ PACHACUTI-YAMQUI: *Antiquities of Peru* (1613)

Right:
Cerro Sechín: One of the stone slabs representing a warrior in ceremonial attire and brandishing an axe.

metry and geometrical precision; also like the *Lanzón* the main vertical figure represents both the "downward" — in the standing personage holding a staff in each claw-like hand — and the "upward" — in the monstrous-masked feline and snakelike features that project from the top of this personage's head. Above this principal figure are four images in which we may see a linear rather than a circular indication of the four cardinal points. The custom of depicting in a rectilinear series elements that in reality are laid out in a circle is particularly common in American Indian art. It was the key element, as we shall see, in the composition of the frieze of the Gateway of the Sun at Tiahuanaco, itself a politico-social offshoot of the same chain of mystical beliefs. As for the origin of the chain, there is an increasing tendency to look to the formal language used in the works of Middle American Indians, who indicated the cardinal points and natural phenomena with complex zoomorphic and anthropomorphic images: several analogies have been traced, particularly with the Olmec culture.

We have chosen to concentrate on the two most striking creations at Chavín, but the Castillo has also yielded numerous other stone fragments — slabs decorated with bas-reliefs of the greatest finesse of design, representing animals, masks, and decorative motifs. Similarly, al-

Cerro Sechín: This view gives a good impression of how the terrace walls were lined by a procession of figures. The fallen stones had only heads carved on them; these were originally stacked three-deep and alternated with the full-standing figures.

Left:
Cerro Sechín: This detail of one of the figures reveals a simplification of the lines and gestures that suggests a link with the advanced stage of Chavín sculpture.

Right:
Cerro Sechín: This single slab has two human heads carved on it.

RELIGIOUS POEM

With gladdened mouth,
with gladdened tongue,
today and again,
this night,
thou shalt call.
Fasting,
thou shalt sing with the voice of a bird
and who can say whether,
in our rejoicing
in our gladness,
from any part of the world,
the creator of man,
the omnipotent Lord,
will listen to thee?
"Hey!" will he say to thee.
And thou,
wherever thou may be,
and thus forevermore,
without any other Lord but him,
thou shalt live, thou shalt exist.

JUAN DE SANTA CRUZ PACHACUTI-YAMQUI: *Antiquities of Peru* (1613)

though the site at Chavín de Huantar appears to have been the prime mover of the period, remains of monuments have been found at Asia, Cajacav, Parash, and other sites in the region. At Kotosh, in particular, not far from Chavín, recent excavations have brought to light two rectangular temples with trapezoidal niches; one is known as the "crossed-hands" temple, from a relief of the clay lining of the interior; the other is known as the "small-niches temple." Kotosh is an older site than Chavín, but it seems that some of the elements at Kotosh belong to the Chavín horizon. Another center having affinities with Chavín — both in its carvings, its pottery, and its triple-terraced pyramid — is Kuntur Wasi, in the valley of the Jequetepeque River.

Cerro Sechín

Of all the remains contemporaneous with and similar to Chavín, perhaps the most puzzling are the sculptures of Cerro Sechín in the Casma Valley along Peru's coast. The bas-reliefs (discovered by the Peruvian archaeologist Julio Tello in 1937) belonged to a temple complex consisting of two rectangular terraces, one on the other, and linked by a central stairway. The upper terrace was lined with a clay plaster and decorated with zoomorphic figures similar to the feline motif of Chavín. But the lower platform and the stairway were lined with slabs of stone, embedded vertically in the ground and bearing incised figures: most of these are of full-standing men in profile, wearing distinctive loin-cloths

and headpieces and carrying weapons. Alternating with these were smaller stones, more or less square blocks, which were piled two or three on top of one another; these two had incised or bas-relief carvings, but only of human heads — definitely suggesting head-hunters' trophies. As an ensemble, these carvings probably represent a processional scene in which a group of victorious warriors return from battle with their defeated enemy and offer them as sacrifices to their gods.

Stylistically, these Cerro Sechín carvings are so unique that they present serious problems when it comes to dating them. The site offers various indications that it belongs to the Chavín horizon, yet the feline motif is certainly not predominant here. Some archaeologists would thus date it early in the cultist period, before the influence of Chavín de Huantar had time to take effect in this area. Other archaeologists, on the contrary, date Cerro Sechín to the late Formative Period, seeing in the work affinities with still later, classical styles. Other students step back from the stylistic details and view Cerro Sechín in architectural terms, emphasizing it as a monument covered with plastic imagery: this then links the work with Middle American sites, and some even go so far as to suggest parallels with the row of relief figures, known as *Los Danzantes*, at Monte Alban, in Oaxaca, Mexico. But in any and all cases, the Cerro Sechín sculptors worked confidently with their own technical precision, stylistic manner, and thematic variety.

San Agustín: The two monolithic figures in the foreground guard the entrance to an underground temple, one of many such in this extensive site in Colombia.

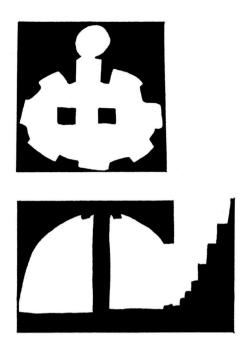

Tierredentro: A ground plan and cross section of one of the many subterranean tombs in this main area of Colombia.

Right and on following pages:
San Agustín: Three of the typical monolithic statues with the intense expressions and mixed anthropomorphic-zoomorphic features characteristic of this extensive area. The one on pages 40–41 is at the entrance to a subterranean temple-tomb.

HYMN TO VIRACOCHA

O Viracocha, power of all creation!
That this may be man,
that this may be woman, so didst thou say.
Holy Lord,
who hast made all the upsurging light,
who art thou?
Where art thou?
Might I see thee?
In the upper world,
or in the lower one,
on one side, on the other,
where is thy throne?
Let me hear thee say only "Hey!"
From the immensity of the heavens,
or from the earth's seas,
where thou hast thy abode.
Pachacamac, creator of man,
thy slaves, with their impure eyes,
wish to see thee.
When I am able to see,
when wisdom has come to me,
when I know how to give the sign,
when I know how to reflect,
thou shalt see me, understand me.
The sun, the moon,
the day, the night,
the summer, the winter,
are not free,
but proceed in order:
they are marked,
and arrive at the stipulated time.
Where, to whom, didst thou send
the glittering scepter?
"Hey!" Say no more than this to me,
listen to me,
while as yet
my strength is not
gone.

JUAN DE SANTA CRUZ PACHACUTI-
YAMQUI: *Antiquities of Peru* (1613)

The Equatorial Cultures

Whatever the particular links between such sites as Cerro Sechín and Monte Alban, it is evident that successive migrations and individuals had certainly introduced — whether across the Isthmus of Panama or by sea — elements of the Meso-American culture that were being re-elaborated, with many original variants, by many Andean communities. Likewise, whatever the exact relationships between such sites as Chavín and Cerro Sechín, it can be said that by the cultist period, the Andean culture stretched in a virtually unbroken line from Colombia and Ecuador down to Chile and even into Argentina. We have been, and shall be, concentrating on the peoples of the Central Andes because of the climax there of a technology and state organization that supported a true civilization. But the peoples of the Northern and Southern Andes also developed their own cultures — working with various farming techniques, building irrigation projects, carving and dressing stone — and although they tended to lag behind the peoples of the Central Andes in many respects, they deserve some consideration.

In Colombia, for instance, after the phase marked by shellfish-eaters and food-gatherers who lived in villages along the sea and around lagoons — roughly 3000 to 1000 B.C. — the first farming communities began to develop (as at Momil). Later, after the fifth century B.C., more advanced cultures — such as those of Tumaco and Calima — began to develop in the sub-Andean valleys. One of the two main archaeological areas of Colombia is that of Tierradentro — west of the central range, in the upper Cauca and Magdalena rivers — a culture distinguished by the many subterranean tombs dug out of the rock in this region. These tombs, circular and oval, were entered by spiral stairways; the main chambers were supported by pillars; they had niches in the side walls, painted decorations based on geometric motifs, and some walls and ceilings with relief carvings.

But the major archaeological zone and culture of early Colombia is that centered around San Agustín, a village situated at an altitude of more than 5,330 feet in the upper valley of the Magdalena River. This area was a junction between the central and eastern regions of the Andes, and as such was heavily frequented: it is hard to know just how populated it was since, as always, all traces of the mass of people's residences, made up of fragile materials, have disappeared. What is left in the area are the remains of the religious and mortuary structures — large artificial mounds with temples, subterranean temples and tombs, slab-lined tombs. And in association with these — at the entrances to the temples, as caryatids supporting the roofs, on the floors of tombs, and in the general area — have been found hundreds of sculptures. Most are carved from volcanic stone, although some are carved in the beds of streams themselves; they range in height from a couple of inches to nearly ten feet — monolithic statues, some human, some animals, some mixed; boulders carved in the shape of heads; stones carved with reliefs: a veritable sculpture gallery.

The exact dates and sources of these works are not known, but their stylistic links with the art of Middle America and with the rest of the Andean cultures appear evident. They look backward in time to the archaic motifs, they look across to Chavín de Huantar, they look ahead to Nazca and Tiahuanaco, but whatever the literal relationships, the San Agustín sculptures stand as a monumental canon of Andean art.

Ecuador does not offer anything as spectacular in the way of sculptural or architectural remains as does Colombia, but its people participated in the same general developments as its neighbors, with several known variants. The earliest settlements date from approximately 7000 B.C., about the time of the coastal settlements of Peru; by about 2700 B.C., such sites as those of El Inca, east of Quito, and Valdivia, indicate the Ecuadorians were in the early farming stage; by the Formative Period, agricultural cultures such as that of Chorrea had further developed. The Ecuadorian peoples tended to build large earth-mound tombs, and they excelled in ceramics and goldwork. By the time of the Inca and the Conquest, the Manteño culture in the central coastal zone had attained a high degree of community organization, attested to by terracing and irrigation systems.

The Southern Highlands

The village remained the fundamental unit of the political and productive system throughout the Andean territory, from Colombia to the southern tablelands. (The only difference was when one group — specifically, the Inca — came along and imposed a pyramidal political and economic structure on this foundation.) Variations of village life, however, appeared. Thus, one of the major sites of the late Formative Period is the complex at Chiripa, on the Bolivian side of Lake Titicaca. There a community built itself fourteen rectangular dwellings in a circle around an open court; each house had double walls — the base of small stones in clay, the upper part of mud bricks (adobes) — and the space between the walls was used for storage. These houses also had another unusual feature — sliding doors. Despite such sophisticated details, though, village life must have remained rather basic at this time.

The main ethnic groups of the southern Andes — the Diagutis, Atacameñis, and Araucanians — lived in farming villages along natural waterways; in case of threats, they took refuge in specially fortified places. Other groups in the area, however, practiced artificial irrigation with canals. The Diagutis' political organization was also relatively simple, based on the local groupings and only forming larger alliances temporarily in time of war. A higher degree of organization was shown by the Araucanians, who, by the time of the Spanish Conquest, had joined together in a federation of the five territories — three of the Mapuches, one of the Pehuelches, and one of the Huilliches. But even then, the small village communities were composed of huts — rectangular, round, or rectangles with apses — which provided shelter for one or more families.

The Classic Period

In the years from about A.D. 200 to 600, a major transformation of culture occurred in the Central Andes region, particularly along the Peruvian coast. These centuries experienced a flowering of artistic styles, the development of farming techniques (such as vast irrigation systems and terracing projects), and the mastery of crafts such as ceramics, metallurgy, and weaving (so much so that the period is sometimes called the "Mastercraftsman Period"). There were several locales where the classical cultures flourished, and regionalism was evident, with nothing quite like the Chavín horizon — that is, a complex of motifs permeating all the sites. However, parallel with this regionalism came a tendency toward social stratification and social organization common to all regions. One feature of the political developments of this period was that the federative organization between contiguous valleys preceded the formation of larger cities. This reversal of the expected process came about because the individual valley villages, before they got around to uniting and developing, began to converge on certain central sanctuaries, and it was these pilgrimage centers that then became the basis for later federative "capitals." Of the several dominant cultural-territorial units of the Classical Period, two will most interest us: the Mochica along the northern coast, and the Nazca of the south coast.

The Mochica Culture

The Mochica culture centered on the Moche River valley, virtually in the middle of the coastal strip of northern Peru that included the valleys of the Pacasmayo, Chicama, Viru, Santa, Nepeña, and Casma rivers. Perhaps the most striking memorial of this culture, and one of the more valuable remains of the classical period, is the Mochica painted pottery, with its scenes of the day-to-day life, its portrayals of nature, and its mythological personages. Close study of these subjects has allowed students to learn not only about specific characteristics of the art and culture of the Mochica people but also about certain fundamental elements that were to be taken up again by other Peruvian peoples in the centuries that followed. One of the reasons this kind of projection may be done — interpreting later developments on the basis of the Mochica pottery — is

Right:
Mochica Art: This clay statuette of a warrior shows the realistic details, the expert coloring, and the skill in portraiture that distinguish Mochica ceramics (particularly the pottery), the most varied and polished in pre-Colombian Peru.

Page 46:
Mochica Art: This small ceramic represents two fishermen in their reed boats.

Page 47:
Huanchaco: These modern reed boats are similar to those shown in the Mochica ceramic (at left). Boats of similar materials, although more complex in their structure, are still used on Lake Titicaca.

that the Mochia culture seems to have passed through a process analogous to the two later Pan-Andean cultures, that centered at Tiahuanaco and the Inca culture centered at Cuzco. Out of the numerous flourishing communities that participated in the Mochica culture emerged the political unification of the Chimú culture centered at Chanchan.

The major architectural remains of the Classical Period in the Moche Valley are the majestic ruins of the *huacas* of the Sun and of the Moon. These bear testimony not only to the deep origins of the Andean religious monuments but also call to mind, as the German archaeologist Max Uhle long ago pointed out, the great Mesoamerican monuments. The two gigantic pyramids are located not far from Trujillo, near the Moche River, along the base of a rocky hill known as Cerro Blanco; they are about 500 yards apart on a plain that was once the site of a village. Despite the fact that the structures, built entirely of *adobe*, have been so eroded that they seem to loom up in the desolate landscape like two natural hills, we can still imagine their original appearance.

The Huaca of the Sun has been particularly damaged along its southern side by floodings of the Moche River, but it still stands 135 feet high. It is made up of a platform about 748 by 446 feet, and about 59 feet high which forms the foundation for a seven-step terraced pyramid. The enormous monument was built by leaning a vast number of pillars, each constructed with large *adobe* bricks, against a central nucleus. The Huaca of the Moon rests on a natural rock base and is of more modest dimensions — about 262 feet by 197 feet, and about 65 feet high.

EARLY ANDEAN CULTURES   47

The purpose of this monumental complex is hinted at by the numerous graves — both single and group burials — found in the vicinity of the pyramids; meanwhile, it is possible that the foundation-terraces may have contained the lodgings of the priests. Obviously, then, these structures had some religious function. But this great pilgrimage shrine — like the Castillo at Chavín de Huantar and many similar edifices built by the coastal communities of the Classical Period — had become more than a symbol of cultural, religious, and political unity; they were functioning temples, centers for all the complex ceremonies related to the daily life of the people. It is not easy to isolate the individual structures and fit them into any specific category and assign them a function, but it does seem

that any such structure can be related to some powerful group, as an expression of that group's wealth, prestige, and leadership. Certainly the pyramids at Moche seem to indicate the prevalence of a priestly caste, symbolized by the great gap between these enduring ceremonial monuments and the dwellings of the masses that once were on the plain between them but of which no trace remains.

Various scenes painted on Mochica pottery also seem to confirm the impression of a state organization that made use of practices generally associated with the later Inca culture. Thus a series of messengers depicted as though running — like the famous Inca *chasquis* — suggest an efficient network of roads may have existed. And in general, Mochica

Moche River Valley: The Huaca of the Sun (left) and the Huaca of the Moon (right) are the most impressive monumental remains of the Mochica culture. It has been estimated that some 130,000,000 unbaked bricks, or *adobes*, were used in building the Huaca of the Sun.

pottery has scenes of dancing, fishing, hunting, and other activities that could almost be used to illustrate the pages of the Spanish chroniclers who arrived in Peru many centuries later.

The exceptional continuity and relative unity of certain fundamental motifs in Andean culture also emerge from the celebrated "revolt of the objects" fresco, which was painted like a frieze on the walls of rooms at the top of the Huaca of the Moon at Moche. The fresco includes a number of scenes representing common everyday objects — shields, darts, etc. — that have been endowed with human arms and legs and seem to be in the act of "revolting" against human beings. Men are being stabbed by their own weapons or taken prisoners by the tools they themselves have invented. The significance of this scene has been rightly interpreted as that of a "last judgment" — in other words, a period of darkness, or *tutayaopacha,* which characterized the interval between the setting of one sun-age and the birth of a new one. It was believed that in such a period, humanity would be destroyed by its own creations, as nature returned to the primeval chaos that introduces a new, slow phase of civilization and a new race. As a result, the cataclysm sees both the unleashing of natural agents — such as winds, earthquakes, floods, and plagues — and the rebellion of man's own artifacts. This alliance, which is renewed each time one of the world's ages passes into another, has been viewed as one of the most characteristic expressions of Inca sacred cosmology and the primary source of religious and state organization of the Andean agricultural communities.

The fundamental ritualistic structure of Inca thought also finds its roots in this glimpse into the eschatological beliefs of the Mochica people. Writing in the seventeenth century, Poma de Ayala divided Inca prehistory into four ages separated by cataclysms; a fifth cataclysm would put an end to history, once and for all time. During each of these four "solar eras" *(intiphuata),* man learned little by little to make use of natural forces, to dominate them, and to bend them to his own ends, until he reached the maximum of civilization permitted to his potential. Then the cycle was broken, the sun set, and during a period of darkness humanity was destroyed. The aspect of this concept that most concerns us here is that the end of the world spells primarily the violent end of a hierarchical order that had been slowly built by man through the subjugation of nature, the transformation of its products, and the pyramidal organization of society itself. In this complete disruption, everything inferior rebels against everything superior and issues forth victorious.

The excessive sacral hierarchy to be seen in pre-Inca culture, therefore, has the ultimate aim of subjugating as resolutely as possible the irrational side of society as well as nature in its various forms. So it is that in Mochica art — the most realistic and faithful in representing everyday life — the chief ingredient in the dynamism of forms and techniques is precisely the determination to dominate, through means of faithful artistic reproduction, the succession of ages and the passing of time. The phenomenon that most directly confirms and reflects this intention was the widespread use of the urn-portrait in Mochica pottery, a full-fledged duplicate of socially prominent personages.

In architecture, too, no confusion between the work of man and that of nature was possible, precisely because it was necessary for the work of man in shaping matter to hold chaos at bay as much as possible by "putting to sleep" the occult energies that could kindle rebellion. Although this concept is contrary to the Inca attitude toward art and other elements of their civilization, it does help to throw some light on the Inca world. The Mochica realm, which presents a number of organizational characteristics that we will find again in the Inca empire, represents the most perfect example, in Peruvian territory, of a state based on the absolute predominance of a caste of priests-chiefs over a mass of vassals. The tremendous economic development of this state resulted essentially from the exceptional irrigation system, which comprised an intricate network of canals. The water tapped from local rivers was channeled into vast desert areas by colossal installations such as the Ascope aqueduct (pages 55–56), which were 50 feet high in places and ran 4600 feet. All this required great discipline, both in the conception and in the execution.

Moche River Valley: A view of the front of the Huaca of the Moon, as seen from the Huaca of the Sun.

Right:
Huaca of the Moon: The panel at left has drawings of the typical animals and plants that decorate parts of the temple. The panel at right shows some of the figures in the so-called revolt-of-objects frieze, in which various objects have been endowed with human features.

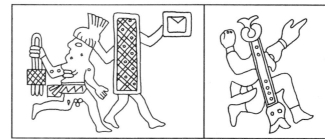

It must also be said that the building materials used by these Mochica people determined to some extent the general shape of the edifices and the spatial layout of the cities, by facilitating the development of well-defined structural and decorative techniques. The Spanish word *adobe* has been adopted to designate unbaked bricks dried in the sun, and it was this material that was used all along the northern coast for the framework and body of the great pyramids and monumental edifices. Another Spanish term, *tapia*, indicates an unbroken wall of masonry, especially those relatively thin walls obtained by compressing clay into special moveable molds on the construction site itself. Unlike *adobe* bricks, the *tapia* forms a compact structure without interstices; if necessary, stones were blended into it to make it more resistant. Unlike *adobe*, too, *tapia* was not used exclusively in the coastal area but also in the Andean highlands.

The ability of the edifices along the coast to resist the weather, however, was mainly due to the extremely dry climate — indeed, an almost absolute absence of rain — as well as to the great thickness of the clay walls. The outer surface of the clay masonry offered numerous opportunities for decoration, either with bas-reliefs or by painting. Decorative motifs were added — particularly in the post-Mochica (Chimú culture) period — by using molds in which the clay was compressed, so that when set up on a wall it would become part of it, later being lined with stucco and painted. This gave rise to the strips with geometrical or heraldic motifs that characterized the gaily colored decorations of the coastal structures.

At Maranga, for instance, on the central part of the coast, near Lima, a

group of artificial mounds reveals the presence of a wide-ranging concentration of terraced monuments. The most characteristic of these is the so-called *fortaleza,* made up of three concentric walls of *tapia* and stone connected to the center by radial walls. Five other constructions — *adobe* pyramids, flawlessly aligned and cemented — make up the main ruins of Maranga. The most impressive pyramid, 164 feet high, has a foundation platform 3200 feet by 1600 feet. The last level of the southern pyramid supports the so-called Maranga Palace which is decorated with geometrical reliefs. Many of these pyramids, like those in the southern area along the coast, contain burial chambers in their bottom layers; these pyramids also reveal some subsequent enlargements around a central nucleus, as is evidenced by the discontinuity in construction and the different sizes and shapes of the *adobe* bricks.

The most important ceremonial site of the coast — that of Pachacamac — was located at the mouth of the Lurin River, a short distance south of Lima. This was a key position in relation to the various coastal cultural areas, and as such was destined to become the main religious center of all Peru. At Pachacamac, the most ancient pyramid (which, according to tradition, hid the oracle grotto where the wooden idol, finally destroyed by Pizarro, was kept) rested on a foundation once attributed to the Classical Period; it actually belonged to the post-classical period (that of the Tiahuanaco culture); in the Inca era, this pyramid was flanked by the Temple of the Sun. The oldest pyramid, constructed of small *adobes,* was painted on the outside in gay colors, with a yellow, pink, or green background, and with large figures of human beings and animals (mostly fishes and birds) and vegetables — all presenting direct analogies with Mochica art.

The residential quarter at Pachacamac, although quite subordinate to the religious edifices, was of some interest. The typical dwelling, which was entered from the roof, was modeled after the traditional coastal type. Meanwhile, the natural maze of alleys and lanes that would normally connect one section of the quarter to another was here replaced by dividing walls that served as footpaths. All in all, there is a sense of regularity, rigidity, and imposed confinement, not unexpected in a society where the masses were kept firmly under control by the religious and political hierarchy.

The Nazca Culture

The main Classical Period culture of the southern coast of the Central Andes region was the Nazca Culture, noted for its superb textiles (page 58) and its brilliantly colored ceramics (page 59). These were made by a people whose cities have vanished; indeed, unlike the Mochica people, the Nazca people hardly seem to have cared about building public structures, religious or otherwise. What we know of these people, therefore, we have learned from their extensive graves and their contents. It appears that much of the energies of the Nazca people was devoted to the preparation of these tombs and the burial objects, evidently as part of some extreme extension of the ancestor worship we noted as an early Andean tendency. The woven textiles, in particular, are considered among the finest in the world — in the technical skills involved, in their artistic designs and colors, in their sheer variety; furthermore, many of the fabrics seem never to have been worn, but were woven specifically to be buried. But although certain individuals were undoubtedly honored by more elaborate burials, there does not seem to be the great gap between social classes as we have seen in the Mochica Culture.

Another particularly intriguing aspect of the Nazca Culture is to be found along the southernmost section of the coast. There is to be seen — since their discovery by airplane viewers — a monumental gallery of earthworks (pages 60–61). They tend to fall into two types, although they are evidently related in some way. One group are lines — some up to five miles long — straight, zigzag, curved, or forming geometrical figures. The other group are figures, most looking like weird emblematic animals. All these works have been "engraved" in the land by digging away the dark crust of the earth — sometimes to a depth of one yard —

and then banking the removed material against the exposed ditch of the lighter subsoil.

There is some evidence to suggest that the plain lines served an undetermined astronomical function or at least a kind of astronomical symbolization, but the figures appear to be exalting some particular totemic "species." Possibly each of the emblems corresponds to a given social group, an *ayllu,* at the same time symbolizing its recognized founder. But everything about these gigantic figures remains speculation — including their exact date; many of the figures do, however, seem similar to those on Nazca pottery. In any case, we find ourselves confronting an altogether extraordinary leap beyond conventional dimensions. The figures were worked into the landscape in such a way as to become part of it, so that the landscape was converted into a backdrop or setting, and the work of the human hand was immeasurably enhanced by the surroundings. (Although there is no place in this region where anyone could have stood high enough to get any overall view of these works: in this sense, the makers could never have "enjoyed" their handiwork and it must have been performed for the gods above.) Perhaps like the Mochica — and later Inca — need to subjugate nature, this was another instance of a ritual taking-of-possession; perhaps, too, it was bound up with ceremonies held when the members of diverse political and social groups assembled for periodic ceremonies of renewal.

Paracas Art: This woolen fabric is from the Paracas necropolis, a site on the coast near Nazca with a culture closely related to the Nazca culture. The figure of a monstrous divinity, with mixed zoomorphic attributes, was depicted in Paracas textiles with extreme adroitness and in vivacious colors.

Right:
Nazca Art: Two double-spouted jars with the complex zoomorphic imagery typical of the classic Nazca ware.

Above:
Nazca Art: A figure of a monstrous divinity, typical of many portrayed on Nazca pottery and surprisingly similar to the central figure represented on the Gateway of the Sun at Tiahuanaco (page 75).

Below:
Paracas Art: Drawings of two monster-figures typical of those depicted in the fabrics of this culture.

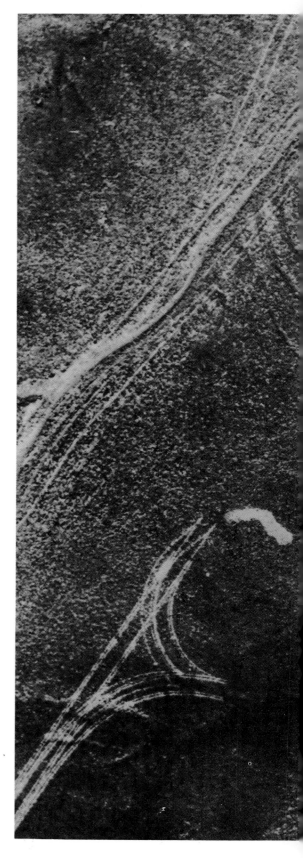

Nazca Art: Drawings of some of the gigantic figures engraved along the southern coast and attributed to the classic Nazca people. These are mainly zoomorphic — based on insects, birds, reptiles and other animals that are presumed to have had some totemic significance, possibly linked to family clans, or ayllus, *for the people who went to such trouble to make them.*

Nazca Art: An aerial view of some of the actual figures "engraved" in the coastal desert by the Nazca people. They are so large that they can hardly be appreciated as figures on the ground, and it is only modern man, with his airplanes, who has seen them like this.

Tiahuanaco: The Site and Its Culture

The Mochica and Nazca cultures are recognized as two of the "pure" classical cultures, but there was another culture that was developing simultaneously with them, one that was destined to play a more expansive role in Andean culture in general. This was the Tiahuanaco culture, which takes its name from the site at an altitude of about 13,000 feet in the southern highlands of the Central Andes, about twelve miles south of Lake Titicaca, in present-day Bolivia. There is great variation in the dating of the monuments at this site, some authorities placing them in the

Classical Period, others in the post-Classical; we incline toward the latter dating. In either case, it is generally agreed that the first phase of the Tiahuanaco culture was confined to this site and its immediate area.

In its second phase, the Tiahuanaco culture spread so widely that it became a truly pan-Central Andean horizon, like the Chavín horizon of an earlier period: a complex of various elements found at many sites. In this phase, the Tiahuanaco culture virtually absorbed the Nazca culture of the south coast; and it spread into various parts of the central and northern regions, where it at last merged with local cultures. This second phase of the Tiahuanaco culture marks it as belonging to the Expansionist Period, which is thought to range anywhere from A.D. 600 to 1100, or even as late as 900 to 1200. This period was characterized by an evidently aggressive expansion of certain peoples, if not through outright warfare, at least through imposed political organization. In the case of the Tiahuanaco culture, in fact, it seems quite certain that no organized people or army went forth from Tiahuanaco and conquered other peoples or regions. Rather, what was involved was a cultural complex and a strong religion that spread from this center and permeated the culture of other peoples. Tiahuanaco, in fact, seems hardly to have been a city, but a ceremonial center; and there has been a general tendency to think of another place, Wari (Huari), in the Mantaro Valley of the central highlands far to the north of Lake Titicaca, as having played an active role in transmitting the Tiahuanaco culture to other places and peoples.

The Tiahuanaco culture horizon, whoever was responsible for disseminating it, was characterized by a number of elements, including a particular type of polychrome pottery, two distinctive shapes of vessels, certain textiles, and several motifs (such as stylized human figures, the puma, condor, and snake heads) that recur in almost all the media of the time — weaving, stone-relief carving, painted pottery, and wood-carving. The Tiahuanaco culture is also characterized by its handling of stone in its structural and design functions; at times the stones reached enormous proportions, yet they were always shaped with a distinctive simplicity. In general, the Tiahuanaco style might be described as a "geometrical period," both in relation to the Inca culture of the future and in its treatment of the motifs of previous cultures.

The classic stone architecture and carving of Tiahuanaco is to be seen, of course, at the monumental ruins of Tiahuanaco itself, a complex built mainly — if not solely — for ceremonial functions. Here, architectural structures and sculptural design conjoin in a powerful yet refined megalithic technique. The largest unit on the site is the Acapana, a stepped-pyramid (now partly destroyed) that was actually built over a natural mound. Close to this is a large, almost square enclosure with some of the large upright slabs and smaller blocks that once formed the walls: this area is known as the Calasasaya. Leading off one side of this, entered by a stairway of six megalithic slabs, is a sunken inner court; the walls of this court have numerous "trophy-heads" embedded in them, recalling the architecture of Chavín de Huantar. There are various sculptured statues about the complex, including the one known as *El Fraile* ("the friar"), as well as remains of aqueducts, a large platform (with carved seats and monolithic portals), and several other constructions. But undoubtedly the most striking and most renowned of the remains at Tiahuanaco is the portal standing near one corner of the outer wall of the Calasasaya — "The Gateway of the Sun."

The Gateway of the Sun

The Gateway of the Sun, perhaps the most celebrated Andean monument, consists of one block of andesite, cut so as to produce a massive gateway, about 10 feet high, 12½ feet wide, and about 20 inches thick. The top of the portal, like a kind of architrave, has a facade almost entirely carved with figures and faces in a series of panels. At the top-central position, and dominating the gateway, is the figure of the main personage, protruding because of its more pronounced plastic treatment. He is represented frontally, his arms symmetrically extended at his sides, his hands grasping staffs; these may be merely ceremonial, like scepters,

Tiahuanaco: One of the great monolithic statues inside the Calasasaya, with features characteristic of the last period of the cultural-religious center near Lake Titicaca.

although the one in the right hand has been interpreted as a spear-thrower, while that in the left may represent a stylized quiver. The trapezoidal head is surrounded by a headdress from which radiate nineteen appendages; the top one has a human countenance, and the others represent either the heads of pumas or ornamental discs. Five more discs hang from under the chin. And most suggestive are the stylized "weeping" eyes, a frequent motif in the art of the Tiahuanaco culture horizon.

The garb of this figure has a belt or skirt adorned with six trophy-heads at the bottom; he is further decorated by a series of ornaments hanging over his shoulders and across his chest, all repeating the motifs of the heads, pumas, and condors. The treatment of the figure, in which parts are in full relief and others only superficially engraved or merely outlined, suggests that the body was conceived of as unclad; it appears to be reproducing an image-idol of wood that was originally covered with rich ornaments, mainly gold plaques. Symmetrically arranged on both sides of the central figure are forty-eight small bas-relief figures of warrior-attendants, each with a scepter-staff in his hand, and shown in profile as they press forward to pay homage to the central figure. These attendants are arranged in three rows, with eight in each row on both sides of the central figure. Those in the middle row wear a mask representing the condor, while those of the upper and lower rows have human features. All forty-eight figures wear headdresses, are richly ornamented, and are endowed with wings and tails. Below these three rows is a row of fretwork, executed with great finesse, enclosing fifteen heads, shown frontally and similar to that of the central figure.

Tiahuanaco: The monumental stairway leading to the Calasasaya; in the background is the statue seen in the previous illustration.

Tiahuanaco: The Gateway of the Moon, a
monolithic portal similar to, but smaller and
simpler than, the Gateway of the Sun.

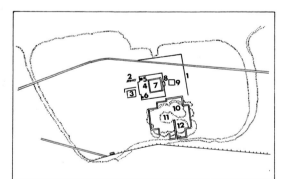

This frieze of the Gateway of the Sun constitutes an important document of the transposition into stone sculpture of decorative techniques and motifs belonging to other media. The archaeologist Julio Tello demonstrated that the forty-eight images of attendants were essentially only two figures, the one with the human face and the one with the condor mask. The faces and the masks are arranged as mirror-images on either side of the central figure, and we may assume that the sculptor used a kind of "stencil" that he applied to the stone on one side, then reversed for the other side. Once the profiles of the attendants were outlined, the artists executed the bas-reliefs by cutting away the background; the impression is of figures that were applied to a smooth surface, almost as if they had been added by the use of a mold.

This most unusual technique can be connected with both the art of weaving — where we also see the precise geometrical repetition of identical figures against a uniform background — and, with more obvious architectural sources, the technique used to decorate *adobe* walls. Again, these walls have "printed" figures similar to those of fabrics, as is to be seen with certain structures along the Peruvian coast (notably, as we shall see, at Chanchan). We might also emphasize a third probable motivation behind this sculptor's technique as well as his choice of materials: the frieze is believed to represent a series of small gold plaques that hung around a sculptured idol — all reproduced in stone here. Whatever influenced the sculptor of this frieze, he seems to be pointing toward two traditions. There were the coastal cultures, where decorations were imposed on the walls of structures by molds or where surfaces were painted.

Tiahuanaco: The sunken inner court, a rectangular ceremonial area surrounded by a wall with stone heads embedded in it.

Right:
Tiahuanaco: A large sculptured monolith within the sunken inner court.

And there were the highland cultures, where structural decorations usually consisted of plaques — at first of stone, eventually also of metal — applied to the bare stones.

The mass of literature — not all of it accurate in its descriptions or its conclusions — on the Gateway of the Sun is now so great that it is not easy to find one's way in the labyrinth of the often contradictory or fascinating explanations of the subject of the frieze. But a close analysis of the various motifs, both compositional and stylistic, should enable us to define the cultural ambience and some of the meanings — at least those central to other artistic manifestations of the Andean cultures. One student of the Andean cultures, for instance, has succinctly summed up all of the more reliable interpretations of the frieze as follows: the religious approach, which takes the central figure as a divinity (most often, Viracocha), to whom the attendants are paying homage; the political approach, according to which three different social groups are appearing before the majestic figure of the sovereign; and the ritual approach, which interprets the positions of the forty-eight figures as traditional for the rep-

Tiahuanaco: One of the stone heads embedded in the wall of the sunken inner court.

There are other nations that say that when the deluge came, all people were destroyed except a few who escaped to hills, caves, or trees; and that these were very few but they began to multiply; and that, in memory of the first of their race who escaped to such places, they made idols of stone, giving the name of him who had thus escaped to each *huaca*. Thus each nation worshiped and offered sacrifices of such things as they valued. There were, however, some nations who had a tradition of a Creator of all things. They made some sacrifices to him, but not in such quantity nor with so much veneration as to their idols, or *huacas*. But to return to the fable, they say that the Creator was in Tiahuanaco and that there was his chief abode. Hence the superb edifices worthy of admiration in that place. On these edifices were painted many clothes of Indians, and there were many stones in the shapes of men and women who had been changed into stone for not obeying the commands of the Creator.

CRISTOBAL DE MOLINA: *Fables and Rites of
the Incas* (1570–84)

resentation of a ceremonial dance, with the participants disguised in masks, wings, and tails.

The fact is, as we intend to demonstrate, none of these interpretations, taken by itself, furnishes a satisfactory explanation for the scene, because we know with sufficient certainty that these three aspects of the public life of the Andean peoples were so closely linked together that there would be no way for a sculptor or his contemporaries to distinguish among these different spheres of activity when confronting such monuments or their decorations. Having said that, though, it is important to understand how the unitary vision of a society was based on a hierarchy, which constituted the basis of all power and all authority, and how this social vision was achieved, both in reality and in artistic imagery. To do this, we must break down the gateway's bas-relief into its principal parts, so as to assess it as a "universal" synthesis of a creative attitude toward a society and its relationship with history, nature, and the divine.

We have already examined the distinctly religious feature of the Andean Indians' symbolism in perhaps its earliest and most intense embodiment, the *Lanzón* of the pre-classical center of Chavín. That sculpture, a mixture of diverse zoomorphic elements, placed vertically like a weapon hurled from heaven into the very center of the Castillo, indicates an absorption of the spatial mysticism in one sole image, totally encompassed in the mythical-religious context, like some idol separated from the other parts of the construction, belonging to a different, purely social, emotional sphere. As we move on into the Classical Period, we might consider the variety of figures (called "chimerical") employed as a motif in the Nazca culture; of mixed animal and human characteristics, often interlaced in a most adroit fashion, these appear on the painted pottery and textiles of the Nazca people. The links with the Chavín culture are evident. For example, the Raimondi stele, also found at the Castillo, is interpreted on the basis of a similar repeated imagery of superimposed heads typical of the Nazca culture. The figures of the Nazca decorations appear to take on, according to the circumstance, every possible feature stemming from the mixture of human nature with the most varied animal forms, without ever singling out an original figure.

In many of the Nazca picture-compositions, however, elements emerge that seem to refer directly to a role of "command." The human figure, seen frontally, is often heavily decorated with complicated headdresses, ceremonial garments, trophy-heads, batons, scepters, and other symbolic elements that identify it with the head of the community, who in particular circumstances can take on the prerogatives set aside for divinities or, in a subordinate way, even identify himself with the divinity.

Some of these Nazca figures, in which the countenance plays a dominant role, seem to be the direct inspirers of the central personage of the Tiahuanaco frieze. Their feet are reduced to two small triangles; their half-outspread arms hold two scepters or staffs; their attire is adorned with trophy-heads. The social and political role of these Nazca figures is not clear, but every detail seems to indicate the representation of "supreme power" through the conventional symbols and the ceremonial insignia. These elements already clearly denote a position of political dominance alongside that which is purely religious and can be interpreted in the same way as is the central figure of the Tiahuanaco frieze. This latter figure, however, can be interpreted still more clearly by its vestments, which appear to be purely ceremonial and are similar to those of the minor figures in the gateway frieze. And it is primarily the presence of these latter figures that puts the whole frieze in its wider context, now that the precedents have been indicated.

We might start by noting that the regal figure of the Tiahuanaco frieze — shown frontally, as is typical of a divinity, and dominating all other elements of the gateway — is essentially repeated fifteen times by those figures in the very bottom row of the frieze. This central figure, therefore, represents the first and principal of the sixteen manifestations of authority in a multiplication that calls to mind the many-headed monsters of other Andean cultural areas. As for the act of homage this figure is receiving from the other forty-eight personages, this seems to further assure us that it is the likeness of a divinity as well as of the sole

Tiahuanaco: The Gateway of the Sun, seen as it stands in relation to the remains of the outer enclosure of the Calasasaya.

HARAWI

Two doves that one day loved one another
in sorrow languish, sigh and weep.
An adverse fate, like a dark, dismal, screaming
   wall,
keeps them apart.
One of them, lost,
separated from her equal lover,
stands all alone amid the stony heights,
heavy-hearted, terrified by her immense pain.
While the other weeps over the image
of his equally beloved,
in his delirium already seeing her dead.
"Oh where, my dear one, are thy beauteous
   eyes?
Where thy breast *my* breast adored so,
and thy heart, thy joy-drinking heart,
thy mouth red as the *achancaray* [a flower]?
Atop the silent, lofty peaks he sheds lonely
   tears,
ranting, raving, and crying aloud,
till there is no breath left in him, till in agony,
his gaze, sweeping out over the wilderness,
   asks:
"Where art thou, then, sweet, my beloved?"
And even as he sings, already half-crazed, he
   falls,
suffering still, shudders, and dies.

Ollantay (I:5)

70   THE ANDES

Tiahuanaco: The Gateway of the Sun, perhaps the most celebrated and most discussed of all pre-Inca monuments. Made of one large piece of andesite, it stands ten feet high, is twelve and one-half feet wide, and about twenty inches thick. *(See jacket.)*

head of the state. In a later period, the Inca were to succeed in creating a synthesis of politics and religion, blending the two main sources of their authority, one terrestrial and one supernatural, into the figure of the king-Sun. The divine king — according to some sources, the ingenious invention of the Inca leaders themselves, who aimed at making their authority autocratic while freeing themselves from the excessive influence of the priests — is the incarnation of the Sun, and as such is to be worshiped, so that at one and the same time we have a state religion and a state governed by a god.

It would seem, then, that we may accept, at least in this general sense, the attributes of the Tiahuanaco figure as a similar example of an authentic fusion of religious and civil authority. And if we cannot say a great deal that is certain about the most ancient Andean cultures or about Tiahuanaco, we can find many elements in Inca-Cuzco ceremonial life that help us grasp some of the meanings of the Gateway of the Sun frieze, thus revealing certain relationships between the realm of the Titicaca highlands Indians and the Inca dynasty.

The chief festivities of the Inca were dedicated to the sun, particularly in its rising, which was awaited in religious silence and then celebrated during the day with elaborate ceremonies. Of exceptional interest to us here is the major political festivity, that of the *Raimi,* during which the participants celebrated primarily the harmony between the empire and the natural cycle of seasons, between the Inca king and his subjects. We know this, for instance, from the description provided by the Peruvian chronicler, Garcilaso de la Vega, in a passage underscoring the political-religious role played by the Inca: "This festival, while it exalted the Supreme Sun, also aimed at paying tribute to the Inca. . . . On that day, the Inca himself would be in Cuzco (unless impeded by war or illness), because it was a day when the Inca, as scion of the Sun, was called upon to preside over the main religious ceremonies. Thus, taking the place of the High Priest, he himself offered the maximum sacrifices." The regal identification with the supreme god appears to be linked with the sun at Tiahuanaco, too: this would confirm the name given to the monumental portal almost instinctively by nineteenth-century archaeologists. Probably, too, it was the sun in its rising phase that was being worshiped by the local Indians; in this case, the central figure of the frieze would also assume a precise spatial role — indicating the east.

The fifteen minor figures in the bottom row of the frieze may indicate as many positions of the sun on the horizon in the various seasons of the year. Then again, considering as months the twelve central elements of the fretwork, the fifteen figures may indicate the central and preeminent position of the sun on the day of the June solstice, with respect to the length of the solar year. Both these interpretations suggest that the figures represented frontally — that is, facing outward — are situated outside the terrestrial space and at an infinite distance along a circular horizon. The flat surface of the bas-relief would thus be a particular spatial version, conceived in accordance with a precise conventional code, of a scene unfolding in time and, contemporaneously, a linear representation of a radial structure. This spatial convention becomes still more evident if one examines the group of the forty-eight small figures shown in profile — situated, that is, in accordance with a particularly widespread artistic convention, in terrestrial space.

To identify them further, we shall turn again to the account that Garcilaso de la Vega gave of the Inca *Raimi* celebration:

The *curacas* [local chieftains] and governors who flocked to the festivities all came clad in their finest attire. Covered with gems, gold, and silver as they were, they looked more like statues than human beings. At the same time, there were others who were completely masked. Some, like the terrible Herakles, appeared at the celebration wrapped in the skin of a great cat, with their own heads hidden beneath that of the beast. Still others fastened immense black and white condor wings to their backs. And whether disguised as cats or condors, they went around pretending that they were not offspring of human beings but of those animals. Others covered themselves while at Cuzco with horrible, terrifying masks. And standing out among these were the *curacas* of the northern coastal region. In addition to masking themselves, they jumped into the air and shouted like lunatics, creating an uproar and muttering senseless words. They also made a great racket with all sorts of noisy instruments, thus endearing themselves to the masses. At the same time, there were some who painted their titles of nobility and the coat-of-arms of their provinces on their chests, brandishing sundry types of arms, from lances to daggers. They also carried paintings of their various exploits, every one of them in honor and defense of the Inca, on their clothing, their heads, and elsewhere. A multitude of odd-looking people would be playing musical instruments, singing and dancing right behind them. And these *curacas* did not attend the festivities by chance, for their presence was envisioned by the ceremonies. In fact, all the *curacas* of the empire took part, and if one of them for some serious reason could not come to the *Raimi*, he would send a son or brother in his place, so that he might participate in the most important festival of the year.

Could it be that the *curacas* here described in this Inca ceremony are the direct descendants of the forty-eight figures of the frieze of the Gateway of the Sun? To begin with, the number of the figures, while it appears to be related to some ceremonial dance, may also correspond to the number of local chiefs of the various parts of the "state" of Tiahuanaco. Indeed, in this frieze we may be seeing the prototype of the *Raimi* festival in a more rigidly ceremonial version, reduced to the essential elements of its politico-religious significance and shorn of the "color" so effectively described by Garcilaso. The garments lined with precious ornaments, making the *curacas* look "more like statues than human beings," are evidently the same that were worn by the personages of Tiahuanaco, transplanted into the sculptured stone, where they became more like ritual images than individuals. Thus the central personage represents not so much the king as a man decked out in his ceremonial robes, as a sculptured likeness adorned with the robes of the Sun.

We also see a direct link between some of the other motifs of the gateway's frieze and the Cuzco festivities — especially in the disguises of the pumas and condors. All the attendant figures on the frieze, in fact, have condor wings attached to their backs. Some also have facial masks imitating this regal bird, while the puma disguise is confined, at Tiahuanaco, to the small decorative heads that adorn the garments. The custom of brandishing weapons also appears to repeat the gestures of the Tiahuanaco attendants, who hold a sort of scepter or spear-thrower.

As for the posture of the richly clad figures in the frieze, this may be seen as representing a particular "step" in the dance. But it is probably no mere coincidence that the motion was "frozen" at this point, for in addition to being arranged in three rows, the figures are symmetrically divided into two halves converging toward the center, a situation that this pose indicates. So that this converging movement also indicates a tribute to the central figure — who, as we have suggested, probably represents the rising sun-god at the moment of maximum splendor — in an attitude of both independence and worship. One can even find a precursor for this motif in the series of *chasquis* on the Mochica vases, where the figures are depicted as running one behind the other as they carry their messages throughout the region. The centripetal movement of the Tiahuanaco figures thus also bears a meaning that transcends the ceremonial dance; it indicates the thronging of the local chiefs to the social center of the state, where the divine head resides. As we shall see in the organization of the Inca empire, each *curaca* represents a well-defined region, indicated with the particular position he occupies and measurable in the distance from the capital and in his position with respect to the cardinal points.

In the Inca culture, as we shall also see, we can trace all the main organizational attitudes of the capital and the empire to the use of what may be called the "polar coordinates" model. So, too, in the gateway frieze, we may conclude that an analogous subdivision — taking into ac-

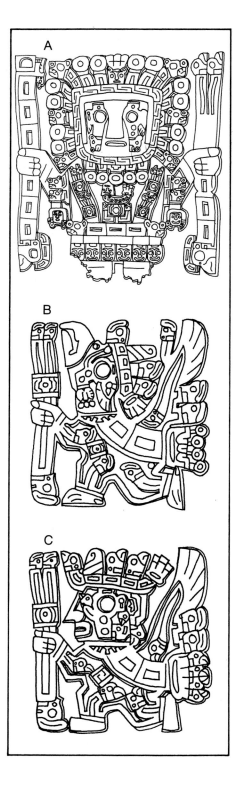

Tiahuanaco: Drawings of details on the Gateway of the Sun
A) *The central figure of the priest-god-king*
B) *The condor-masked figure repeated in the second row of the carvings*
C) *The human-headed figure repeated in the first and third rows*

Tiahuanaco: The central figure of the frieze of the Gateway of the Sun. Here may be seen the three rows of attendants on each side, paying homage, with the bottom row of fretwork.

count the distance and direction of the individual *curaca*'s territory, and the fact that he belongs to either one "half" of society or the other — is at the basis of the particular position of each figure. If, as is highly probable, the solar idol indicates the east, the two halves — each made up of twenty-four *curacas* — are subdivided by an ideal east-west line, joining together in two distinct, complementary parts, north and south, each one under an "arm" of the Sun-king, who represents their union and "hinge." The upper half of society should be that under the right arm (on the left as we view it, and corresponding to the north); the lower half of society is under the left arm (on the right, corresponding to the south).

This interpretation is solidly rooted in the concept of society and its classes manifested by whatever we know of the early Andean populations and brought to the fore in the Inca world. The division carried out by the mythical Inca founder, Manco Capac, among the inhabitants of the capital, Cuzco, and reflected in all the other cities of the empire, was based, for example, on the partition of those who lived in the upper part of the city and those who lived in the lower. The first Inca, in fact, sanctioned

that "the inhabitants of the upper part were to be considered his first-born offspring, while those of the lower part were to be considered his second-born. This was established in the image and likeness of the human body, which has a right arm and a left arm: both are precious and necessary to the body, but the first — by nature and by custom — is always the stronger and more capable of the two. . . . Later on, all the other cities in Peru were planned in line with this subdivision, in the districts and quarters alike, according to the people who lived in them and their descent. The aristocrats thus called their quarter *Haynansuyu* [upper quarter] and the plebeians called theirs the *Hurinsuyu* [lower quarter]."

In the Tiahuanaco frieze, the right arm and the left arm of the social "body" appear perfectly balanced. Situated ideally to the north and the south (and in Cuzco the demarcation line between the upper and lower parts ran southwest to northeast), the two halves represented by the *curacas* probably indicated all the main directions of space. The number of *curacas,* in fact, is derivable from a geometrical subdivision of space concentrated around a central point — in groups of two, four, eight, and sixteen. As we shall see in connection with the organization of the Inca empire, there was always a precise correspondence — in terms of a number as regular as possible — between the subdivision of time and space, and the distribution of social groups.

To sum up, then, we can consider the Gateway of the Sun frieze as a representation in a ritual scene of the organizational principle of the state, which had its center in the city-sanctuary of Tiahuanaco. From a technical-artistic standpoint, we are almost certainly confronted with a copy of a scene executed with different, less resistant materials: a wooden or stone idol clad in princely ceremonial attire and surrounded by small golden plaques representing *curacas* in ceremonial garb. From the iconographic point of view, the various features of the sculpture and the typology of the personages mark an intermediate stage between the Classical Period and that of the Inca — the rather rigid geometric style so typical of the Indians of the Titicaca highlands. From the iconological standpoint, the scene probably represents an annual ceremonial dance, ancestor of the Inca *Raimi* festivities in honor of the sun and hence of the monarch. The political meaning includes not only the homage of the *curacas* to the supreme sovereign but makes it possible to recognize a number of essential features of the ritual concept of the ramifications of society and the state. The most compelling of these elements is that regarding the division of the scene into two halves and the ideal distribution of the various personages around a circle in accordance with the cardinal and intermediate points of the universe. As for the central figure, it is extremely probable that we are already at Tiahuanaco witnessing a king identified with the sun, in the double function of high priest and supreme chief.

The Kulpi and the Chullpa

We have mentioned in passing that the Indians of the Andean highlands excelled in working with stone, whether in the details of smaller carvings or in the architecture of large-scale monuments. The techniques became so widespread and so refined that we can hardly avoid stonework from this point on, but here we might take a slight excursion to examine two particular variations. They are both somewhat peripheral to the major lines of cultural development, and they have been dated anywhere from the end of the Tiahuanaco-Expansionist period to post-Tiahuanaco times known as City-Building Period. One of these types of stone construction is known as the *kulpi;* it was used throughout the region to the northwest of Lima, in the central part of the slopes bordering the Pacific. The *kulpi* has often been compared to the other type of stone construction that here concerns us — the *chullpa* of the Lake Titicaca region — but direct reciprocal influences seem to be ruled out, not only by the great

Tiahuanaco Art: This polychrome pottery in the Tiahuanaco style is characterized by the sharp geometrization of forms that recalls the Nazca ware.

distance between the two areas but also by the different purposes of the constructions: the *kulpis* were dwellings, the *chullpas* were tombs. But if these two types of architecture developed independent of one another, it is doubtless true that both derived from a common and long-standing Andean tradition of building structures at least half-underground — a practice that we noted as early as the site at Huaca Prieta.

The *kulpis*, small edifices probably intended for only one family, were generally circular in shape, occasionally polygonal or rectangular. They were constructed with a hollow pillar in the center of walls that spread outward slightly toward the top; the roof, slightly sloped, was made of large slabs of stone that rested on the central pillar and protruded somewhat over the outer walls. There was a stone floor at ground level, but inside the pillar a ladder led to the underground chambers dug out beneath this floor. The first subterranean chamber usually had small niches and hiding places for offerings and cult objects; below this, a second chamber served as a crypt where the remains of ancestors were preserved in animal hides. Usually the only entrance to the *kulpi* was a single trapezoidal door, three feet high — and facing east. There were also more elaborate *kulpis*, where the door was preceded by a deep, high niche. But all doors, internal niches, and windows were of the same trapezoidal shape. The more complex *kulpis*, however, no longer had their burial chambers below them but in a separate structure some distance away.

These dwellings were frequently gathered together in such numbers as to constitute villages, some of considerable size, as is shown by the remains at such places as Chiprac, Anay, and Ruprac. Indeed, at such sites the presence of temples and various other public areas suggests virtual urban development. And the Peruvian *kulpi* evokes other associations. It can be considered, for instance, a rendition in stone — including the slab roofing — of the type of coastal dwelling made of *adobe* and with roofing of vegetation; these dwellings, of course, have not survived, but they are familiar from the painted designs of local pottery. But for all the relationships of these *kulpis*, they must be placed in a special context to understand the true reciprocity of their main component parts.

For the *kulpi* is essentially a type-variant of a dwelling used throughout South America, a structure in which were represented, in accordance with a precise hierarchical concept, the succession of the three regions of the cosmos — the celestial, the terrestrial, and the subterranean. These are the places inhabited, respectively, by the gods, by man, and by the dead, and they are situated one on top of another along a vertical axis that unites them. (Even the *adobe* huts of the coastal peoples often had a central support on which the roof rested.) An analogous cosmological concept guided the construction and use of the great pyramids of the Andean Classical Period; in these, the underground burial areas were covered by terraces symbolizing various "worlds" that progressed to higher levels until the highest point was reached, where the temple of the divine stood.

In the *kulpi*, however, it was the life of the individual — or, rather, of the family — not of the community, which aimed at connecting itself with the fundamental structure of the world, and through a continuity that was both spatial (via the architecture) and temporal (through the burial of ancestors in the sacral levels of the dwelling). The subterranean world communicated with that of human beings through the central pillar-ladder, yet was separated from it by an intermediate zone, where offerings for the dead were placed and idols propitiated. The stone floor was the actual separation, and above this rose the pillar supporting the roof-vault, which represented the sky. The accepted symbolism also attributed to the pillar the function of "fixing" the position of the house in relation to the cardinal points; moreover, with the entrance at the eastern side, the horizontal axis was east-west in relationship to the solar rising point.

The *kulpi* affords us a valuable example of an architectural concept that all but disappeared with the development of the great theocratic com-

Drawings of two kulpis. *That on the left is the simpler type, while the one on the right is the larger type, with the trapezoidal windows and the little covered entranceway.*

Cross sections of two types of chullpas. *That on the left is the simpler, with the single-domed burial cell; that on the right is a variation, with two interior burial chambers, one above the other.*

Right:
Sillustani: The remains of this circular burial chamber, or *chullpa*, from the Lake Titicaca region reveal the highly finished stonework used for such structures by Inca times.

Following pages:
Sillustani: These are the remains of other, cruder *chullpas* found in the same area.

plexes. These latter concentrated in the sanctuary alone both the function of establishing a relationship between the territory (or physical space) and the cosmos (or celestial space) and the representation of that total cosmological system in the ramifications of the structures. But it is the survival of the simple *kulpi* dwellings that clarifies the basic elements of the religious-monumental architecture of the Andean region. Quite early, as we saw with the Castillo at Chavín de Huantar, it was to be the temple that embodied the needs of the community, and worship tended increasingly to be transformed from a private activity to a public one. In this light, the *Lanzón* of the Castillo plays the same role as the central pillar of the *kulpi* or other private homes. The common dwellings, meanwhile, tended toward simplification, becoming a virtually uniform hut built altogether above ground: the onetime profusion of significance was lost to the family unit and absorbed by the central structures.

The *kulpi*, in fact, seems to be a relatively late version of a type of dwelling that had previously been found in numerous other Andean localities; but elsewhere by this time, the various parts of the private dwelling had taken on the role of architectural types in themselves or had become parts of more complex public buildings. Thus we have seen in the great San Agustin complex in Colombia the underground temple-sanctuaries with their roofs supported by pillars. But the other particular variation of stonework in the Andean highlands that most concerns us is the mortuary edifice known as a *chullpa*. The *chullpas* are found in the region of Bolivia around Lake Titicaca — at such places as Sillustani, or near the Oyuni lagoon, or at Maucca Llaita. Although many of the *chullpas* were built during the time the Inca had annexed this region, the oldest date back well before this. Most archaeologists assign the name "Chullpa culture," in fact, to the City-Building phase of the Colla, the Indians who inhabited the Bolivian highlands; this would place the *chullpas'* decisive phase sometime between A.D. 1000 and 1440.

As mentioned, too, some specialists stress the similarities between the Bolivian *chullpas* and the Peruvian *kulpis*, but we prefer to see them as cases of architectural forms sharing a common source — namely, the subterranean dwellings and tombs of the early Andean peoples — but as having developed in different ways and employing techniques that are only superficially similar.

The *chullpa* is generally round in shape, occasionally square or rectangular. The most imposing ones have diameters of twelve to fifteen feet and attain heights of over thirty feet. The exterior walls of some are formed of standard-sized stones, smoothly rounded and accurately joined; others are of rougher stones, but neatly constructed. A band in relief, protruding a few inches, divides the vertical wall from the roof, which imitated the cupola of a vault — and was intended to symbolize the heavens. The roof was made of stone and mud of great thickness, and indeed the bulk of the *chullpa* was solid; it was really like a compact artificial tumulus, built over a small sepulchral cell. This burial chamber was entered through a tiny door — facing east, of course — and within were a number of niches; this inner chamber was also covered with its own pseudo-dome.

The *chullpas* were used by several families, and in their size and construction were much more important than the dwellings of the families. Such a specialization indicates that these structures belonged to a type of social organization in which the tomb was no longer only a private concern but a status symbol; it had become the symbol of the position enjoyed by the various lineages within the community, and as such it had to be more ambitious and enduring than the dwelling of any individual family.

Northern Highlands Cultures

Simultaneous with the major lines of cultural development that we have been tracing, other centers of artistic and architectural achievement were flourishing. One such is called the Recuay culture, named after the site where its most distinctive pottery was found; the Recuay culture was confined to the valley of the Callejón de Huaylas — only twenty miles from Chavín de Huantar. The Recuay culture is variously assigned to the true Classical Period — which would make it a contemporary of the Mochica and Nazca cultures — or to the Expansionist Period, and thus a contemporary of the Tiahuanaco culture: in either case, it seems to be dated at about A.D. 600 to 900.

The Recuay culture is particularly noted for its ceramics, characterized by the so-called negative (or lost-color) painting technique: a resistant coat of liquid clay is applied to make the desired design; the exposed areas are then treated by one of various ways, after which the clay resist is removed to reveal a "negative" image. The distinctive motif of Recuay ceramic decorations was a highly stylized monster based on a jaguar, but there was considerable variation in the designs as well as in the shapes. The upper parts of vases often have a "frieze" running all around, with scenes of ritual sacrifices dominated by priests. One vase is topped by a small model of a terraced temple with sculptured heads embedded in its walls.

Such subjects confirm the impression that the Recuay culture was a politico-religious society typical of the kind that flourished in relatively confined valleys. The chief known center of the culture was Wilkawain (near Huaraz) and it is dominated by the remains of a sanctuary that rose

Recuay Style: This pot with the anthropomorphic head and the geometric designs is typical of this ceramic style.

above the common dwellings. The edifice was rectangular (fifty-two by thirty-five feet) and had three stories (to a height of thirty feet); it originally had a sloping slab-stone roof. Outside, beneath the roof line was a sort of cornice that suggests the frieze element of the Castillo at Chavín; lower down and embedded in the walls were stone puma-heads — calling to mind those at Chavín and Tiahuanaco. Inside, each story had seven main rooms, and there were various staircases, ventilation shafts, and other elements.

Wilkawain suggests a social organization centered on a sanctuary and a class of priests acting as guides for a homogeneous agricultural territory. As such, it suggests that the Recuay culture was slightly behind its contemporaries, the classical cultures of the coast. It was, in effect, a survival of the theocratic-ceremonial society long before developed in the nearby Marañon Valley and centered at Chavín de Huantar.

Another isolated center in the northern highlands was Marca Huamachuco, near Cojamba in the Chicama Valley. This was a fortified center occupying the top of the Cerro del Castillo; it was enclosed by a defensive wall of stone and bricks more than thirty feet high. Inside were long, narrow dwellings of two or more stories, constructed of stone. This is probably a late site, belonging to the City-Builder period.

Marca Huamanchuco: Plan of the archaeological complex. Situated on a series of adjacent hills, the main fortified center was on Cerro del Castillo, at the right.

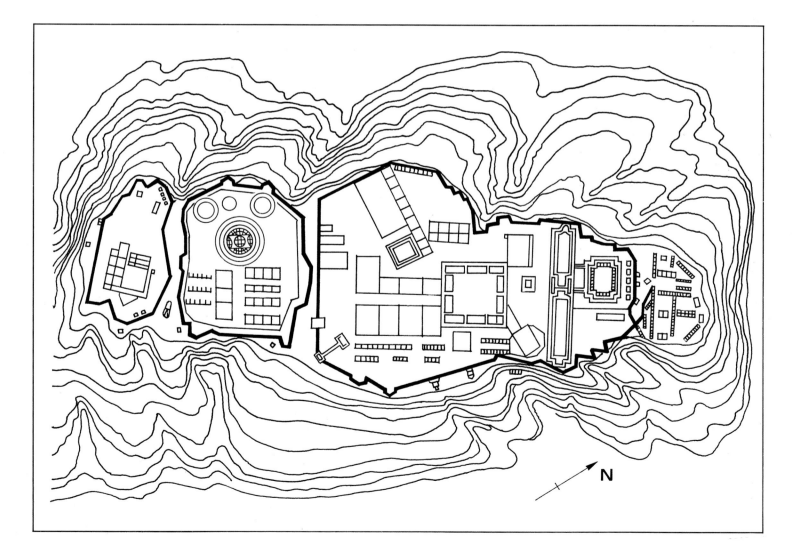

The Chimú Culture and Chanchan

The Mochica people who had so flourished in the Classical Period seem to have become increasingly aggressive, expanding their culture from the original valley centers until they controlled the whole northern coast. When the Tiahuanaco culture was at its most expansive, the Mochica culture seems to have temporarily withdrawn, but in the years after 1100 a modified form of the Mochica culture began to appear. This is known as the Chimú culture, and as the Chimú people asserted their control along the northern coast, a type of political state developed, flourishing from perhaps 1350 to 1450 — that is, until the Chimú state was incorporated into the Inca empire. During its peak years, the Chimú "kingdom" stretched about as far as Tumbez in the north, and south at least to Paramonga; incorporating the coastal valleys, densely inhabited and irrigated, the Chimú state remained a series of isolated peoples — the cause,

Chanchan: This view of part of the imposing ruins of the capital of the Chimú kingdom shows how badly the buildings have been damaged by the elements.

among other things, of the defensive weakness that left the Chimú so vulnerable to the Inca.

Indeed, given its exceptional size, the Chimú state appears to be less an instance of a political organization and more the result of a historical adaptation to conditions. It was "supra-regional," yet it remained territorially fragmented and never worked out a concentrated unity. The Chimú system lacked that which became the springboard for the swift territorial expansion of the Inca: the concept of space radiating from one sole "navel" in every direction, and therefore balanced, a continual confrontation between top-level authority, conceived as a unitary principle, and the innumerable peasant communities subordinate to the center through rigid bureaucratic control.

For all its limitations, however, the Chimú state is considered the most extensive Andean economic-political organization prior to the advent of the Inca supremacy and, at the same time, the most complex evolution of the ancient minor-state-units of the coast. And the best way to approach this Chimú state is through its most decisive memorial, the capital of the

Chanchan: Plans of two of the "palaces." The Chanchan complexes, extremely rigid and symmetrical in design, were evidently almost self-sufficient units and inhabited by one upper-class clan and its retainers.

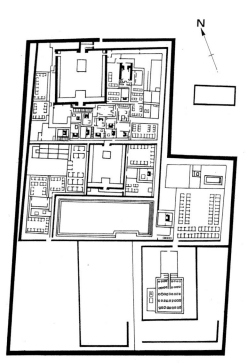

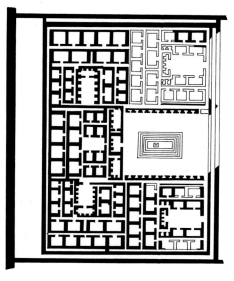

realm, Chanchan. The ruins of Chanchan cover an area of at least six square miles near Trujillo and are considered the most extensive archaeological city of South America. The nucleus of the site consists of ten complexes, or large blocks of structures, roughly rectangular, and each enclosed by powerful walls, most having only one opening communicating with the outside. In the areas between these complexes and in the vast peripheral area are traces of the roads, aqueducts, reservoirs, walls, cemeteries, irrigation works, and other structures.

The ten complexes are sometimes referred to as "palaces," but this is misleading; they may contain palacelike buildings, but "wards" would perhaps be a closer description of these large units. Although varying in details, all share certain features: a reception area; a series of small dwellings usually laid out, in the ancient Peruvian custom, on the three sides of a court, or lined up in a single row or in double rows; a cistern for the water supply; a burial ground; and a pyramid-temple. The most complex of them, known as the Great Chimú Complex, includes a series of forty-

Chanchan: A group of rooms with a trellis-work wall structure. The use of clay throughout — from the basic unbaked bricks to the bas-relief figures on surfaces — allowed for a series of light and shadow effects, giving walls an articulated sequence of rhythms that appear to have been based on textile designs.

five small cells with a narrow entrance at the top of each; these have often been described as prison cells, but they may be no more than storage rooms. Certainly, though, the sense of confinement leads us to imagine that these complexes were like gigantic labyrinths, conceived in accordance with some great design, and in which an entire social life unfolded.

Above all, it is the consistency, the repetitiveness, of these complexes that make the city of Chanchan so suggestive. There is no doubt that a plan, carefully conceived and executed, regulated the great center of Chanchan from its inception, and subsequent developments did not introduce any particular changes. The ten complexes — one adjacent to another and each on a lot calculated as to its size and location — can be considered the residences of distinct class-groups. The fact that all joined together in the same organism indicates that they approved of some political confederation. And, indeed, Chanchan represents a solution to the problem of the urban organization of a capital of a vast confederation, and as such it has both similarities and differences with the Inca

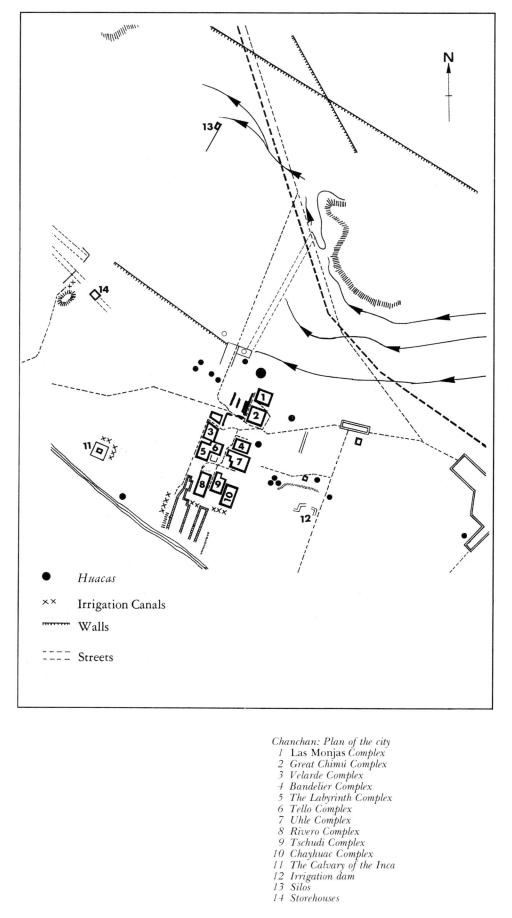

Chanchan: Plan of the city
1 Las Monjas *Complex*
2 *Great Chimú Complex*
3 *Velarde Complex*
4 *Bandelier Complex*
5 *The Labyrinth Complex*
6 *Tello Complex*
7 *Uhle Complex*
8 *Rivero Complex*
9 *Tschudi Complex*
10 *Chayhuac Complex*
11 *The Calvary of the Inca*
12 *Irrigation dam*
13 *Silos*
14 *Storehouses*

Legend for plan:
● Huacas
×× Irrigation Canals
〰 Walls
- - - Streets

N

Chanchan: An interior wall, with molded decorations of fantastic birds.

Chanchan: Interior walls, with the typical
trellis-type structure and molded reliefs.

Following pages:
Chanchan: A wall with a molded decoration
that produces the effect of a tapestry.

Chanchan: An interior of one of the complexes. Visible in the background is one of the walls that enclosed all such complexes.

Chanchan: Drawings of some of the common symbolic zoomorphic figures that were repeated, "carpet style," on so many of the walls at Chanchan.

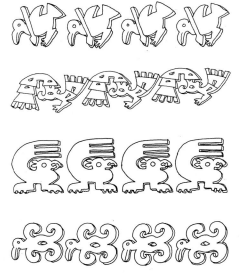

capital at Cuzco. At Chanchan, as at Cuzco, the urban layout was meticulously planned: both cities represent the climax of the traditional regularity of earlier urban installations in the Central Andes, particularly along the coast, incorporating the principles of stereometry, geometry, and monumentality typical of the preceding religious architecture.

The accomplishment of Chanchan was probably the highest organizational stage reached by the populations of the coast, for this was the final phase of the process of association among the various political units centered in the individual valleys. This confederation took place, and not by chance, under the direction and in the territory of the most important culture-group, which for centuries had been established in the basin of the Moche River. What is more, in this new political association, the absolute domination of the priestly class which had appeared side by side with the emergent political chiefs, and had indeed identified itself with their hereditary powers, by now appears to have lost ground to the evolutionary thrust of a class of warriors and state officials — probably belonging to the same relatively few family groups. There are indications that the grouping of different family lineages into core units, none subordinate to others but all on a level of equality, corresponded to the confederation of various upper-class *ayllus,* that oldest and most traditional Andean social unit.

The architectural achievements at Chanchan required a high degree of artisan specialization, and this also showed up in other fields such as textiles, goldsmiths' wares, and pottery. A marked simplification of forms and a reduction of decorative themes was in part the result of the "industrialization" of technical procedures that in the preceding Mochica culture had left considerable leeway for individual interpretation. In the production of ceramics, for instance, many were now made with molds and painting was essentially abandoned; instead, geometrical decorations and plastic imagery followed widely used patterns.

But the most characteristic trait of the Chimú culture was the extensive use — at Chanchan and other Chimú sites — of low-reliefs applied to the walls by molds. Both the outside and inside surfaces of the massive walls were enlivened by enormous regular designs — repeated over and over again, as in a carpet — some geometrical, some profiles of objects or bodies, particularly of a zoomorphic nature. This use of a particularly rich repertoire of decorative stylizations that had been developed by the preceding coastal cultures was now channeled into monumental architectural decoration with all the characteristics of an art reduced to mass production.

This codification of forms and objects seems to have originated in the appropriation by the main power groups of the Chimú of the archaic symbols whose totemic significance had gradually been assuming a mere heraldic meaning in these northern coastal settlements. The individual figures may therefore represent the *pacarina,* the mythical place of origin of every clan, repeated over and over again precisely to indicate the multiplication of the race in a multitude of people who were all alike. But it is clear that by this time these "figurines," reduced to reproduction in one series after the other and used with great indifference with respect to their intrinsic meaning, utterly lost the semantic tension and social value that emanated, for example, from the gigantic figures drawn in the earth by the Nazca people.

In Chimú society, the various social groups were evidently so stabilized within rigid ritual formulas that they were incapable of evolving toward a truly unified political organization. The repetition that itself became the chief motif of the plastic and pictorial decorations of the Chanchan walls reflects the excessive formality and the intrinsic immobility of this society. But it is the layout of the large complexes that provides a still clearer picture of the fundamental nature of Chimú society. These major enclosures were made up of several smaller units, usually walled, and each evidently planned as separate, functioning units and with a rigid symmetry of their own. Evidently they contained particular sub-groups specializing in some well-defined function within the more extensive upper-class enclosure as a whole. This internal segmentation suggests — at least for the larger and more complicated blocks of houses — a total independence, almost as if they were neighborhoods within a city. And in fact, the features typical of urban organization — namely, the separation between the sacred areas, the residences of the rulers, burial areas, quarters for artisans and laborers — are found *within* each of the ten complexes at Chanchan, not on an overall urban scale.

All indications are that this stemmed from an extreme development of hierarchization inside the individual *ayllus.* The state at large then came to reflect this pattern, the obverse side of which was the ineffectual power relationships among the various chieftains of large and distant territories. (It was this latter relationship that the Inca learned how to control so well.) The Chanchan enclosures contain those various elements that made up the separate urban settlements of the Classical Period, although now they have been transformed both in their functions and proportions. The step-style period itself has now passed from its public sacerdotal function to that of something like a private "chapel," set aside for a given group and a given cult. The lodgings of the priests, once so distinguished, are not recognizable inside these Chanchan complexes. The clearcut ritual position of each element that had characterized Andean urban development has come to correspond to the ceremonial-etiquette imposed by absolute rulers.

It may well be that Chanchan was the mandatory residence of the chiefs of the individual "realms" of the Chimú confederacy; if so, the design of the capital reveals that it was more of a loose association than a genuine fusion. This can be explained by the nature of the Chimú territory, made up of a series of valleys, one separated from the other: their basic spatial model was a continual, single-direction series, rather than radiation from a center. If we observe the plan of Chanchan, we are struck by the symmetrical layout of the ten major complexes along the central axis, an ideal median line linking the sea to the mountains and

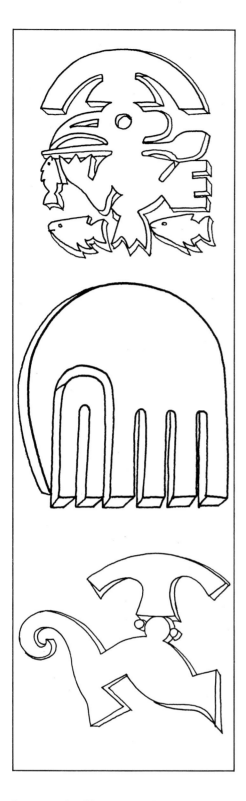

Drawings of molded motifs used in decorating the walls of Chanchan and other Chimú cities.

Left and right:
Chanchan: On the edge of the main group of complexes is the so-called Huaca of the Dragon; the exterior of its walls is covered with a slightly different type of molded clay decoration, as may be seen in these three views.

separating the northern part of the coast from the southern part. Such a layout suggests an initial conclusion: each complex may correspond to a given people or valley, situated to the north or south of Chanchan according to its position along this median line. The distance to the sea might then be thought to correspond to the relative distance between the individual confederate territories and Chanchan. Such a concept of urban design would be similar — allowing for the different spatial context — to the radial relationships between the various "quarters" of Cuzco and the regions that composed the Inca empire.

Another basic analogy between the layout of Chanchan and the structure of Chimú society as a whole is to be noted in the internal arrangement of the individual complexes. Although we have indicated that "palaces" can be a misleading name, in one sense they were royal preserves: there was no space for accidental or individual developments that would aid the general public. Within the city of Chanchan, as at Cuzco, no poor classes were found; only the representatives of power lived in these complexes — and possibly their immediate subordinates. Probably the more humble classes lived in mud huts in the vast peripheral area around the complexes. But the lines between the two main social classes were as decisive and impenetrable as the great walls surrounding the complexes.

La Fortaleza at Paramonga

Among the other monumental complexes of the Chimú state, the one that most stands out for its originality and grandeur is the great fortress, known today by its Spanish name, *La Fortaleza,* near Paramonga; it has given its name to the river valley on the southern frontier of the Chimú territory, the borderline with the Inca state that soon overwhelmed it. This great structure probably belongs to the period just before the final confrontation between the two states in the second half of the fifteenth century; it could not keep the Inca away, however, and in fact they rebuilt at least parts of it after they had annexed this region.

The fortress proper was part of a defensive line that ran from the slope facing the sea, past the fortress, into the interior for many miles, finally joining the first of the Andean summits. Access to the fortress had been carefully worked out on the basis of strategic needs, and included successive portals, various passageways, and guardposts. The fortress consists of three superimposed terraces (with an overall height of about sixty-six feet), built entirely of *adobe* reinforced with pebbles, and occupying the top of a natural rise, or spur. The foundation terrace extends outward with four so-called bastions of varying sizes; they are basically prolongations of the breastwork of the main structure, and have many nooks and crannies, recesses and projections. The diagonal junctures of these several protuberances suggest other Andean defensive structures, such as that at Marca Huamachuco (with its angled bastions on the ring of walls, and its angled internal structures) and the fortress above Cuzco, Sacsahuamán (with the sawtooth shape of its three terraced walls).

At Paramonga, the upper terrace holds the remnants of chambers with niches, decorated with stucco and gay colors (yellow, white, red). This suggests that the distinctly military nature of the edifice did not altogether preclude its symbolic, monumental role — also enforced by its extremely precise construction. The architectural type, moreover, clearly stems from the stepped-style pyramid-temple; those contemporaneous with *La Fortaleza* have also evolved from the absolutely rigid forms to trapezoidal or irregular quadrangle shapes. Particularly illuminating would be comparisons with the Inca Temple of the Sun at Pachacamac, situated in the central part of the coast, a short distance south of Paramonga.

Paramonga: The great fortress built of *adobe* bricks; this view shows the terraced structure, with the bastions protruding on both sides.

Following pages:
Paramonga: The great fortress, with the entrance to the outer enclosure clearly visible in the foreground, right.

Paramonga: This view from above the largest of the bastions shows how it protrudes from the central body of the fortress.

Aside from such considerations, we should note the plasticity of *La Fortaleza*'s structure, which absorbs all irregularities in an "organic" formulation of the relationship between the main central body — organized around the verticality of the successive terraces — and the four lateral protuberances — which almost seem to be more concerned with indicating the diagonal expansion from the center than in functioning as bastions. These and other elements mark *La Fortaleza* as a mountain structure, rather than a coastal structure. As in the Inca cities to come — particularly at Machu Picchu — the design has moved away from the total a priori geometric rigidity, breaking up in apparent freedom to adhere in a natural sense to the least suggestions afforded by the lie of the land. The trapezoid, the triangle, the irregular quadrangle, the steep slope of the walls and the apertures, however expedient in the articulated design of a fortress, bear testimony to a taste that has little to do with the monotonous axial repetitions found in towns along the coast — particularly at Chanchan. In such sophisticated handling of formal elements, the Andean peoples may be considered to have found a way to fit the work of man into nature and to endow it with a vital continuity.

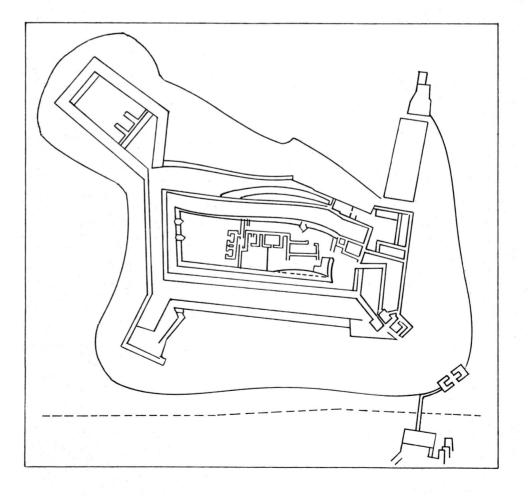

Paramonga: Plan of the fortress.

Chimú Art: This gold ceremonial knife (from Lambayeque, on Peru's northern coast) is one of the most refined examples of the goldsmith's art in the pre-Hispanic period.

THE INCA

Society Under the Inca

In the study of ancient and primitive peoples there is often a tendency to consider elements of progress, changes in style, or the introduction of new technological methods as resulting from invasions or migrations of other peoples. Undoubtedly, contacts between various peoples tend to transmit material culture to expanding portions of the human race. But probably more frequently the most important civilizing factor is experience itself. So, too, the evolution of social organization among many peoples is identical to this development of material culture, and the pre-Columbian Andeans are a classic example of a people responding to their own experience.

The community based on a grouping of villages had a long history in the Andean area, and the system of community life was already so deeply rooted in the culture of its peoples that the Inca had only to build their empire on it. The Inca conquest of these communities thus did not give rise to the same forms of exploitation as had occurred in Europe. Conversely, the Spaniards themselves had to take the Andean community system of production into account in order to control the local populations and to obtain the agricultural products they needed. By the eighteenth century, in fact, the century of the "utopians" in Europe, the most advanced form of the Andean community, the Inca Empire, was even being characterized as "the perfect society," and it inspired philosophers such as Campanella (although he was of the seventeenth century), writers like Jean-François Marmontel, and dramatists like Germany's August von Kotzebue.

It is not easy to pin down the century in which the organization of labor in the fertile valleys of ancient Peru began, but it was certainly at an early date, perhaps at the very dawn of agriculture there, at least about 1500 B.C. The initial communities came into being precociously, aided by the physical nature of the territory and the climate. The narrow fertile valleys were ideal for sustaining small settlements. Neither geography nor nature favored migrations: to the north and south for many miles there was desert; to the west, the ocean; and to the east, the mountains and then the tropical forest. Perhaps certain regions — such as the valleys along the north coast — accelerated and diversified the process of the centralization of power, but in general the basic Andean community arose early and persisted for a long time.

These village communities were, in fact, to become the nucleus of all the historical Andean civilizations, surviving the Inca invasion and the Spanish Conquest. We have already spoken of these communities in connection with the origins of the *huaca,* and we learned that the word for these communities in the Quechua language is still *ayllu.* One of the oldest dictionaries of the Inca language (compiled, of course, after the Spanish Conquest) translates the word *ayllu* as "tribe, people, lineage, family," thus suggesting the several overtones to the word. But finally it is best to think of it as a village composed of several families who claimed to have descended from a common ancestor, whose *huaca* was venerated at the center of the village or in its immediate vicinity. The tendency to

Machu Picchu: The *intihuatana,* a sundial and solar "observatory" carved out of the natural rock at the summit of this Inca city.

remain endogamous while developing patrilinear descent strengthened still more the ties and traditions of the community.

The villages were often surrounded by walls that incorporated the small houses of stone or unbaked brick, possibly even sharing a common roof. At the center of the village was a courtyard; around the walls outside was the cultivated land, the territory, or *marca,* of the *ayllu.* The land, like the dwellings and the food resources, was common property; plots were redistributed for cultivation each year among the various members of the community. It was communal life in its most absolute form.

The communities in the highlands were similar, although they lacked some of the characteristics described. At times, for instance, there were *ayllus* with two or three secondary, dependent villages. In the mountainous territories, where agriculture played a secondary role and the raising of llamas provided the chief means of support, attention had to be devoted primarily to the task of finding the proper pastures. In these areas, scattered, isolated houses did not form small independent communities, but were linked up with other equally isolated homes in administrative communities of relatively large proportions.

The village chief, or *curaca,* chosen in a more or less formal fashion by a council of elders, was an important personage in the community; he presided over the dispensation of justice, the distribution of land, and the administration of common property. This figure of the village chief went through a series of modifications in the course of Andean history; certainly under the Inca Empire, the *curaca* had to be acceptable to the central authorities. (There is some confusion in the use of this and many of the other Indian terms, due to the early Spaniards' confusion, but most modern authorities tend to apply the term *curaca* to the appointed representative of the Inca.)

It is not known with certainty today whether the *curaca* had to cultivate his own land or whether this was attended to by the community. Some students of the *ayllu* reject the theory that the simple peasants had to till not only their own land but also "those of the Inca and the Sun." But it seems quite certain that in the last phase of the Inca Empire, at the very least, the villagers had to work the lands of the *curacas,* the priests of the Sun, and the Inca rulers. The agricultural labor and its produce was one of the forms of taxation imposed by the Inca. In turn, the products of this labor helped to fill the supply-magazines along the highways, and these were distributed in time of famine or war. So it works both ways: if we are to recognize the Inca's ability to provide for the needs of a vast territory, we must also admit that they controlled its labor force.

As for the assignment of land to each member of the community, the criterion described by Garcilaso de la Vega in his *Comentarios Reales* appears likely. The *curacas* supervised the annual rotation of lands among the villagers, and also the assignment to every newly married couple of a *tupu* of land. The *tupu* seems originally to have been a standard linear measurement of about four and one-half miles; as an areal measurement, it came to be about an acre. As each male child was born, another *tupu* was added to the family — and only half a *tupu* for every female child. Although the land was common property and redistributed each year, the rotation had to be flexible enough to take demographic changes into account. The land of people who had died, for instance, was assigned to newborn babies or to newly married couples, who had themselves left land free in their respective families.

Under the Inca empire, there developed several other categories of people, and we shall discuss them in some detail when we come to examine the organization of that empire. Here, though, we might at least mention one particularly distinctive group, because we need to know about them if we are to understand how the Inca put together their empire. These are the *mitimaes,* the populations transferred from one locality to another. The decision to transfer whole communities might be taken after a rebellion or grave acts of insubordination in a territory, or it might be based on the simple desire to exploit the more fertile lands in some region or to undertake major construction projects such as roads. Whatever the motives, it was forced transfer of populations, and the *mitimaes* must have served as a powerful deterrent to any group who considered challenging the ruling Inca, especially since each *ayllu*'s life was so rooted in its local *huaca*.

Origins of the Inca

The Inca themselves left virtually nothing in the way of history to posterity; the renowned *quipu* — the knotted cords — which the Spaniards thought was some form of writing, is now considered to be simply a system of recording numbers for accounts and statistics, based on the various types and positions of the knots. Writing was completely unknown, so that only monuments, painted pottery, and various other artifacts survive to tell us something, if carefully interpreted, about the early history of the Inca.

There are, of course, the various chroniclers — mostly Spanish — who came along after the Conquest and began to record the oral traditions of the Inca. But only a small minority of these men were familiar with the indigenous languages, and when these stories were gathered together — by men such as Vaca de Castro, Pedro Sarmiento de Gamboa, the Viceroy Francisco de Toledo, and others — they came out full of contradictions. (Incidentally, the several early chroniclers who are quoted at any length throughout this volume are identified in the Appendix, page 187.) They were often rich in anecdotes, but they were hardly authentic reconstructions of events preceding the Conquest. They succeeded in piecing together only about one century, really going back only to Pachacuti. For the ruling dynasty itself, there was considerable confusion about which events occurred in whose reign, but out of the various accounts modern students have at least been able to agree on the number and descent of the Inca Emperors.

As for the history of the culture and the Andean people in general, some modern students contend that the stories of the Inca were falsified by the natives employed by the Spanish; other scholars claim it was distorted by the Spanish chroniclers who, filtering it through their own ideology, suffused it with Greek-Roman, Biblical, and Christian-medieval elements. Whatever the many contributing factors, it is hard to find solid facts regarding the Inca and their past. Allowing for this, though, we may examine a representative selection of the major stories, not so much with the idea of providing a simple history as to give some flavor of the Inca, much as we come to understand something of the ancient Greeks by reading the *Iliad* and the *Odyssey*. And just as with the ancient Greek myths and legends and history, we must accept that there are numerous and different versions to choose from.

One version of the origins of the Inca was set down about 1630 by a Jesuit missionary, Anello Oliva. Although it obviously contains many elements of folklore and legend and myth, it agrees in its general outline with accounts of the predynastic Inca in other sources. (For more on Oliva, see the Appendix, page 187).

I had been unable to obtain the slightest information about the origins [of the Inca] from any of the historians, when one day Dr. Bartolomeo Cervantes, canon of the Holy Church in Charcas, presented me with an article on this very subject. The article had been written on the basis of accounts handed down by Catari, who had been a *quipucamayoc* for the last Inca, a post he had inherited from his ancestors, descendants of Ylla, the inventor of the *quipu.*

Catari relates that after the universal deluge, of which the Indians had perfect knowledge and which they called *pachacutec,* the first human beings who arrived in America, either intentionally or because driven there by a storm, landed at Caracas and from this point, multiplying, spread out over all Peru. Some of them settled near Cape Sampu [which is today called Sant' Elena] under the guidance of a *cacique* known as Tumbe, or Tumba, whose good government made the nation prosper.

After reigning for a certain period and desiring to increase the number of his states, Tumbe sent one of his best captains with a large number of Indians to look for new lands, with orders to return at the beginning of the year. But at the stipulated time they did not come back and nobody ever knew what became of them. Indications are, as I shall say a little further along, that they went to populate Chile, Peru, and Brazil.

In any event, the *cacique* thought they were all dead, and what afflicted him most was that, already being old and ill, he could not go look for them.

Shortly afterward, in fact, Tumbe died, after having given orders that a new expedition be organized to go out and look for his men and at the same time discover new territories.

This *cacique* left two sons, the oldest of whom was called Quitombe and the second, Otoya. After the death of their father, these two sons lost no time in fighting with each other, so that they spent their days in great enmity. In order to put an end to this and also to carry out the orders of their dying father, Quitombe decided to leave the country. He soon set out with all those who wanted to follow him and traveled throughout the country until he came to a particularly pleasant plain, where he decided to settle. And it was on this plain that he founded the city of Tumbez, named after his father.

Before beginning his journey, Quitombe had married Leira, who was renowned for her beauty throughout the land. In view of the fact that she was pregnant, however, he left her behind, promising that he would come for her after a certain length of time. Though unwilling, Leira had consented to this because she loved her husband deeply. When her time came she gave birth to a boy, whom she named Guayanay, or Swallow. And it was from this son that the Inca who would become the sovereigns of Peru were to descend.

During this period, Quitombe had sent out expeditions in all directions, both to seek new lands and to look for traces of the men who had been sent out by his father. One of these expeditions, after having made its way through a long stretch of the coast, arrived as far as Rimac [which is today the city of Lima] but the men found no trace of those who had preceded them.

During this period, Otoya, who had remained at Cape Sampu, freed from the obstacle represented by his brother, gave himself up to cruelty and drunkenness. He mistreated his subjects so badly that in the end they decided to rid themselves of him through murder. But Otoya was put on his guard against the plot being hatched and after having tortured to death the leaders of the conspiracy he carried on with his life of debauchery until a group of giants arrived on the scene. The giants took Otoya prisoner and with their mistreatment caused the death of many of his subjects. Not having any women with them, the giants devoted themselves to sinning against nature, until at last, God, enraged, slew every last one of them in a rain of fire. The natives had regained their freedom but they no longer had a chief; Otoya had perished in the prison where he had been kept by the giants.

According to tradition, the giants were so tall that the heads of ordinary men hardly arrived at their knees, and they had come to the locality on rafts made of huge tree trunks. They dug wells of great depth, such as those still seen at Cape Sant' Elena, filled with fresh water. In this area one can still unearth human skeletons of prodigious size with teeth weighing as much as fourteen ounces. I was shown some skeletons so large that I would have found it hard to believe if I hadn't actually seen them. In all likelihood, these giants belonged to the same race as those who once landed in New Spain and whose bones are still to be found in the Tloscala district.

The tradition recorded by the *quipucamayocs* also says that, when the giants were exterminated, a youth of prodigious beauty appeared in the sky, hurling in their direction the flames that were to destroy them. It is probable that this was an angel of heaven.

In his city of Tumbez, Quitombe learned of the ruin the giants had caused in his brother's territory and decided to flee from this imminent danger by setting out to sea on a number of rafts, which he immediately ordered built. On the second day of his journey he landed on an island which he found fertile and richly stocked with fruit. It was also covered with the maize plant, which grew uncultivated. Quitombe named the island Puna and decided to settle there once and for all, without ever returning to the mainland. As time went by, it became self-evident that the island was a particularly dry one, for it never rained there. In the end, Quitombe was compelled to settle in the mountains of Quito, to which he gave his name. Several of his companions continued on to populate the mountains of Charcas and Cuzco.

Quitombe, who was a man of good sense, went to the coastal area to settle near Rimac, in view of the fact that, even if no water should fall from the sky, that of the rivers would be sufficient to irrigate his land. He therefore ordered work to begin on great irrigation projects and had a grandiose temple built in honor of Pachacamac, to whom he offered generous sacrifices. Today one can see the ruins of these near Lima.

Not long afterward, Quitombe died and, in accordance with the custom of his people, was buried in the mountains. He left a cruel, bloodthirsty son named Thome, who invented weapons of a different type and was the first to wage war to subjugate neighboring nations, and in fact these nations were conquered by him.

When Quitombe's wife Leira saw that, instead of coming back to get her at the agreed time, her husband appeared to have forgotten her altogether, her love for him was transformed into hatred. She climbed to the top of the Jancar mountain, accompanied by her son Guayanay, and, kneeling on a stone, tears running down her cheeks, addressed a prayer to the great Pachacamac, supplicating him to wreak vengeance on her husband for having abandoned her. No sooner had she finished than the earth went into a great tremor that was to last several hours, and such a fearful hurricane broke out that one would have thought the very elements had gone to war with each other.

Leira interpreted these signs as a promise on the part of Pachacamac to aid her in taking vengeance, and out of gratitude decided to sacrifice her son to him. She had the boy washed in a fountain and had already laid him out on the pyre and was about to set it afire, when a royal eagle swooped down and clutched the boy in its talons. The eagle then flew off with the lad to an island in the very middle of the sea, called Guayan because of its numerous willow trees.

All this may have been the work of the devil, but it seems to me more likely that the boy was not carried off by an eagle at all but merely ran away to escape the wrath of his mother, who had come to hate him because of what his father had done. To save his life, therefore, he had put out to sea in a canoe and had taken refuge on this island, where he was to remain many years, living on roots and wild fruit.

At last, when he was 22 years old and weary of that solitary existence, he built a raft so that he could return to the mainland, whose mountains he had descried in the distance.

While approaching the shore he was all at once surrounded by a great number of canoes filled with savages dressed in animal skins. The savages took him prisoner and led him to their chieftain, who ordered him to be confined in a well-built hut under good guard, with the intention of offering him in sacrifice on the first festival that came along.

Guayanay was strong and handsome, and news of his capture and his beauty attracted all the local inhabitants, who came in throngs to get a look at him in his prison. The throngs included a young woman of exceptional beauty, called Ciguar, the daughter of the chieftain. The girl was so overwhelmed by the good looks of the prisoner that she at once resolved to make every effort to restore his freedom. She found a way to talk to him in secret and to warn him of the danger, since her father had decided to sacrifice him to his gods on a festive occasion to be celebrated the very next day. At the same time, she promised to run any risk to save him, provided he in turn promised to marry her and take her with him.

When Guayanay accepted the proposal, the girl managed to persuade the guards to let her into his prison cell, where she slipped him a *champi*, a small battle-ax. Armed with this weapon the prisoner

Inca Art: This *kero*, or beaker, made out of lacquered wood, is typical of Inca work in pottery and other minor arts, with its extreme schematization of the decorative figures and designs.

slayed four of the six guards assigned to keep an eye on him. The other two escaped and hastened to their chief to inform him of what was happening. But in the meantime Guayanay and Ciguar reached a canoe that Ciguar had ordered made ready and they took refuge on his island.

Guayanay led his bride to a flower-bedecked meadow in the midst of which he had built a cabin. Standing over the cabin and shading it with its branches was a tree whose branches distilled enough fresh water for their drinking.

The couple settled down and lived there many years, along with their numerous descendants. In fact, it was long after the death of Guayanay that the island was rediscovered.

Thome, son and successor of Quitombe, and hence blood brother of Guayanay, was then reigning in the highlands and in the realm of Quito. This prince, extremely severe, had promulgated a law according to which adulterers had to be punished by being cut to pieces. It so happened that one of his own sons had become guilty of this very crime, and knowing he could expect no pardon, had taken flight in a canoe, along with a number of his companions. His intention had been to allow himself to drift with the current along the coast until his father calmed down. But, driven offshore by a violent storm, he was at the mercy of the waves for two days, at last landing on the same island where Guayanay had taken refuge. The inhabitants of the island numbered about twenty-four and they were governed by Atau, son of Guayanay and Ciguar.

Atau, a name meaning "fortunate one," received the fugitives extremely well. Learning from them of the great expanse of solid land nearby, he decided to go there to settle, for the island no longer produced enough food for its inhabitants. But since by now he had become too old, he had no time to carry this project out. Realizing that he was at the point of death, he called his son Manco to his bedside. Manco was a capable, kind youth of great courage and was then twenty-five years old. Atau took him aside and urged him to leave immediately after his death, to settle on the mainland. Manco promised that he would, aware that he really had no choice in the matter, in that the island, which had a perimeter of one league only, no longer produced enough food and could easily be submerged by a storm.

My Inca, my only Lord,
what a calamity!
My Inca, my only Lord,
the great tree has fallen.
My Inca, my only Lord,
thou wert our day!
My Inca, my only Lord,
thy lovely crown of gold!
My Inca, my only Lord,
thy enemies have taken it away!
My Inca, my only Lord,
thy majesty and thy power!
My Inca, my only Lord,
the memory of them torments us!
My Inca, my only Lord,
there is no heart that forgets
our idolized Inca.

(from the version of Jesus Lara, 1957)

The Inca Dynasty

According to one legend, which attributes divine ancestors to the Inca, the dynasty was brought into being by the four Ayar brothers and their four sisters. Having issued forth from a site known as Pacanectapu, some four miles east of Cuzco, they set out in quest of a place to found their kingdom on behalf of the Sun, their father and protector. The names of the four founding brothers have been interpreted as follows. Ayar Manco means the chief, the one invested with the supreme authority; Ayar Uchu symbolizes the interior of the country, where pepper is grown, for *uchu* means pepper; Ayar Auca means the rebel, the one who resists authority; Ayar Cachi symbolizes the coast, where salt marshes are found, for *cachi* means salt. These references were probably related to the four points of the Tahuantinsuyu, which are often found in Inca mythology. The same can be said for the names of the four sisters. Mama Ocllo means the fecund mother, the woman who takes care of the hearth; Mama Huaco represents the masculine woman who holds responsibility, perhaps a reference to the village-life when it was under a matriarchate; Mama Cora comes from *cora*, the name of a wild herb that grows in the forests to the east; and Mama Raua comes from *saraua*, or maize — Peru's major cultivated plant, raised mainly in the valleys along the northern coast.

The four Ayar brothers went with their sisters to the top of the hill called Huanacauri, and there they sowed the maize the Sun had donated to them. But in no time at all, discord flared up among them. Ayar Cachi was the first to be eliminated. By a ruse, he was made to enter a grotto and an enormous boulder was rolled down to seal up the opening; Ayar Cachi inveighed against his brothers and invoked the god who had created the earth, Viracocha, who transformed him into a condor, thus allowing him to escape from the grotto; Ayar Cachi then flew to the top of Huanacauri, where Viracocha changed him into a rock. This legend is significant, in that Viracocha, a god who appears only in late Inca mythology, intervenes to prevent Ayar Cachi from dying a cruel death but does not alter the course of events as desired by man. Ayar Cachi was eliminated as a historical force, but remained a *huaca*, an ancestor, a funeral totem-monument, the sacred Huanacauri.

Another brother, Ayar Uchu, chose to remain at the side of the *huaca* to dedicate himself to the worship of the Sun and of the creator Viracocha (and in some versions, Ayar Uchu himself then is turned into a stone *huaca*). Ayar Manco and Ayar Auca are left to go on to Cuzco. And note that throughout these tales, the sisters play but a minor role; only

At the top is a drawing of an aryballus, a pot with a pointed base, associated with the Inca. It was used to transport liquids, and the drawing of a terra-cotta statuette, below, shows how the vase was carried on the back, with a cord passing through the two rings on each side of the vase.

Mama Ocllo is predestined to marry Manco and so become the progenitress of the dynasty of the Inca. It is also interesting to note how the entire story takes place in the immediate vicinity of Cuzco, thus confirming the highly sedentary nature of the Inca people.

The next brother to be eliminated was Ayar Auca; he was defeated because he was the rebel and outcast, the one who had to submit to the will of both the gods and of Ayar Manco, the predestined one. According to one legend, Manco and Auca had a staff of gold, given to them by the Sun; the city of the Inca was to be founded wherever this staff, thrown down, would sink into the ground. On the way to Cuzco, Manco threw the staff down again and again, but without success. These fruitless attempts stirred up the contempt of Auca, who wanted to make a try. Manco bore his brother's scorn with patience, until at last the staff cut into the terrain at his feet and disappeared. Now the land where the corn was to be sown had been chosen; it was soft, humid earth, the very kind needed. And at this point, Manco extracted the staff from the ground and with one blow crushed his brother's head. So it was that Ayar Manco became Manco Capac, the founder of the Inca dynasty, with his sister Mama Ocllo, the protector of the family and the hearth. They wore their regal attire covered with gold and were worshiped by the local inhabitants of the place that was to become Cuzco.

Garcilaso tells us that after founding Cuzco, Manco Capac colonized numerous villages in the four quarters of the Inca territory, and taught the people many of the arts and industries. He was succeeded by his son, Sinchi Roca, who embarked on a peaceful expansion toward the Lake Titicaca region, persuading the Puchina and Canchi peoples to submit to the Inca. Other settlements in the area, observing the good administration enjoyed by these two peoples, established ties with the empire. In similar fashion, the third Inca emperor, Lloque Yupanqui, called the "Left-Handed One," is said to have organized an army of six or seven thousand men to establish order in the annexed territories and to have continued the conquest of the region around Lake Titicaca. He met with resistance from the Ayahuiri, but the Inca won the decisive battle; on the site, the Inca erected the Pucara fortress, which was to serve as the base for later expeditions against the Colla.

Lloque Yupanqui then withdrew to Collao, the present-day port of Lima, leaving a large army at Pucara. Shortly afterward, his troops moved to the west of this territory into the ancient province of Hurin Pacassa, as far as the slopes of the central Andes; these lands — approximately thirty-five square miles of territory — were easily pacified because the natives were living in a tribal state, scattered far and wide. Or so we are told by Garcilaso de la Vega. And, indeed, the many feats attributed to these early Inca emperors were probably highly exaggerated versions of what were perhaps no more than the Inca's first contacts with neighboring territories and peoples — or at most, minor skirmishes with local tribes. Manco Capac certainly appears to be a mythical being, and the next several emperors seem more legendary than historical; not until we arrive at Pachacuti in the mid-fifteenth century are we on solid historical ground. For one thing, if we are to believe all the traditional tales, the Inca had defeated many of the Andean people during the early centuries of their emergence; yet there are many reasons to believe that it was only in the last century before the Spanish Conquest that the Inca really imposed their control over such widespread territories.

Again, though, we may read these accounts as expressions of the Inca ideals. Thus, according to reports given to Vaca de Castro, Lloque Yupanqui married Mama Caba and had three sons; the eldest of them, Mayta Capac, became the fourth Inca emperor. Forced into a long-drawn-out war with the Alcabisa — according now to Sarmiento de Gamboa — he put together an army, splitting up his forces under four commanders and devising primitive military tactics. His enemies were obliged to fortify themselves on the top of a hill; in the redoubt, made of stones, earth-clods, and branches, the besieged sheltered their women and children and brought in a supply of food and water. The siege continued for fifty days, until at last — so the legend went — the arrows and stones of the besieged, by the will of the Sun, turned in the air and returned to wound those who had thrown them. The Alcabisa — who in some versions were the Collas — were thus compelled to surrender, but they were well treated by their conquerors. As a result of this victory, the Inca were able to push farther into the southeastern territory, welcomed by the natives who had been informed of the choice made by the Sun during the battle.

Mayta Capac's son, Capac Yupanqui, succeeded him, and as soon as he became emperor, he led his army toward the territory of the Collas in the southeast. This region had for some time been stirred up by the skirmishes between two local *curacas,* Cari and Chipana. When the Inca forces arrived, the two *curacas,* fearful that the powerful emperor might ally himself with one or the other of them, requested his mediation in their conflict. Capac Yupanqui accepted this task with great pleasure; he invited the two *curacas* to his camp, showed them the organization of his army, and explained the wise rules of life followed in the empire of the children of the Sun. Cari and Chipana, exhausted by their long hostilities and admiring the wisdom of the Inca, and also fearing the emperor's power, decided to federate with the Inca empire.

This episode is revealing of a number of elements. For one, there is no question that the *ayllu,* the village community, existed prior to the Inca empire, and that its economic and social structures resisted the authority of the Inca overlords. The theory of the "great federation" often set forth in the accounts of the chroniclers is thus probably true in its general outlines, even if dates and details are wrong. Such episodes also reveal how political, economic, and religious power was conceived of as one unifying force within the Inca empire.

According to Vaca de Castro, the eldest son of Capac Yupanqui and his wife Mama Chuqui Yllpay, daughter of a powerful *curaca* of the Ayarmaca people, was Inca Roca, who became the sixth emperor. His biography is extremely controversial. Garcilaso says he fought against the Chancas, the children of the puma; Vaco de Castro says he dedicated himself primarily to the building of temples; Sarmiento says he married Mama Micay, daughter of a *curaca* of Pataguayllacan and former fiancée of Tocay Capac, the great chief of the Ayamarca. This last version also gives rise to another tale in which the Ayamarca go to war against the Inca; Tocay Capac managed to take the son of Inca Roca prisoner and would have slain the boy but he began to weep blood, leaving his would-be killers astonished and terrified. As a result of this prodigy, the boy took the name of Yahuar Huacac, which in the Quechua language means "blood-weeper." When the young man was eventually ransomed, the two peoples came to terms and made peace. Topay Capac, the offended chieftain, married a sister of Yahuar Huacac, while the latter took in marriage Mama Chizquia, the younger daughter of Tocay. The Inca who had "wept blood" was to remain in Cuzco forty years, bolstering his authority over the various peoples of the surrounding territory; Mama Chizquia bore him six sons, the first of whom was to become the great Viracocha.

The Last Great Inca Rulers

The history of Hatun Tupac, who reigned under the name of Viracocha, becomes confused with that of his son and successor, Pachacuti; but by now some glimmerings of historical facts begin to emerge from the shadows of legends. Viracocha, who reigned around the year 1430, does seem to have instituted the supply-magazines in the villages; he resettled various peoples — the *mitimaes* — in conquered regions; he declared Quechua the official language of the entire territory; he built various roads; and he organized the *ceques,* the system of milestones and border markings that indicated the distances on the highways of the empire. But the chroniclers have many other tales to tell.

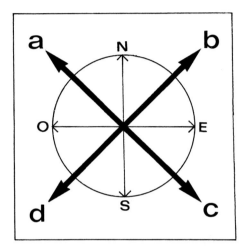

A diagram indicating the relationship between Cuzco, at the center junction of all lines, the cardinal points, and the four provinces of the Tahuantinsuyu — "the joining of the four parts," which is what the Inca called their empire:
a) Chinchasuyu: the northwest region
b) Antisuyu: the northeast region
c) Collasuyu: the southeast region
d) Contisuyu: the southwest region

THE CREATION OF CUZCO

Oh day, king, sun, my father!
"May there be a Cuzco,
may the capable one be
he who measures":
saying thus,
thou hast ordained,
thou hast created.
I must worship thee, I must!
Happy, limpid may life be,
so hast thou said.
Never equaled,
and without bounds may he be,
the one who can achieve all,
the omnipotent one.
And we creatures,
his slaves.

(Transcribed by Cristobal de Molina, 1575)

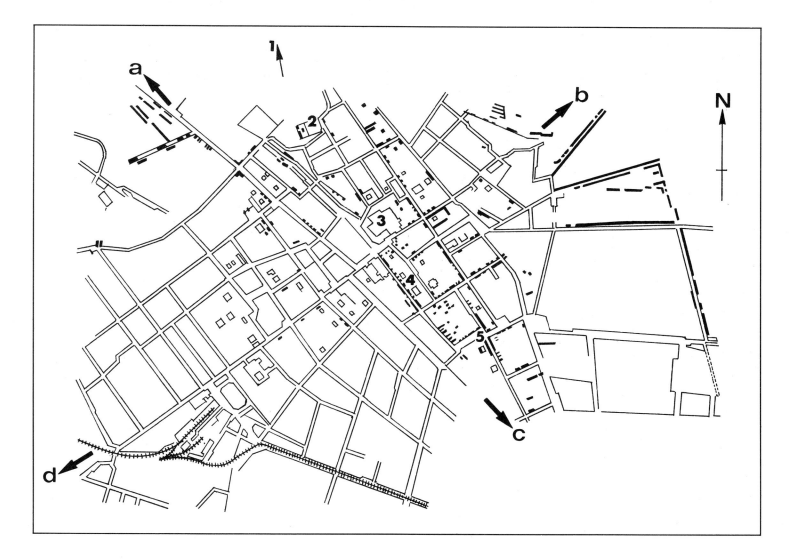

Following pages:
Sacsahuamán: This fortress overlooking the city of Cuzco is the most impressive fortification of the Andes. It is made up of three walls of enormous stones laid out in sawtooth fashion, making it possible for the defenders to strike at attackers from the flanks.

They say that at nineteen years of age, Hatun Tupac was such an undisciplined, rebellious youth that his father Yahuar Huacac sent him to graze herds far from Cuzco. After a few months, Hatun Tupac returned to the royal palace and asked to be received. In the presence of the old emperor, he related that he had dreamed of Ayar Auca, also called Viracocha, "who had come from the sea," and who had warned him of a revolt of the Chanca peoples and their allies in the Chinchasuyu region and at the same time had offered him support and assurance of an ultimate victory. The emperor did not believe the tale of his rebellious son and drove him away. But a few months later he came to regret this; the rumors and then the refugees began to pour in from the mountains around Cuzco. An army of forty thousand armed men, commanded by Anco Ayllo, chief of the Chancas, was approaching the city. Yahuar Huacac, seized by panic, quit Cuzco along with his court and withdrew to the Huina gorge. But the news of the invasion also reached the pastures of Chita where Hatun Tupac was, and soon, arming himself with a lance, he had gathered together the soldiers who had fled and he laid an ambush for the invaders.

Once Hatun Tupac began his desperate battle against the army of Anco Ayllo, others faithful to the Inca began to arrive from the surrounding hills. Word even began to spread that the stones in the woods had been transformed into armed men by the will of Viracocha himself. The Chancas were seized by panic; Anco Ayllo, in an attempt to rally his troops, threw himself into the thick of the fighting and was wounded. The end came as the Chancas surrendered by the thousands. Hatun Tupac reentered Cuzco in triumph, and removing the yellow ribbon worn in his hair by all descendants of royal blood, he replaced it with the red ribbon of the emperor. And as emperor, Hatun Tupac assumed the name of his patron-god, Viracocha Inca.

According to Garcilaso, the natives of what is now Bolivia and of a

region reaching as far as the high plateau of Tucuman (Argentina) subjected themselves to Viracocha Inca, and shortly afterwards the emperor prepared an expedition of Chanca warriors, under the command of his new subordinate, Anco Ayllo, to conquer Chile. But the *quipucamayoc* (mistaken by the Spaniards as court historians, but who probably were limited to keeping accounts) told Vaca de Castro that Viracocha Inca conquered the territories to the northwest — that is to say, in the very opposite direction to that of Tucuman — occupying Trujillo and pushing as far as the Piura River.

Not long afterward, the chief of the northern coastal region, Chimo Capac, a peaceful sovereign of the Chimu, surrendered to Viracocha Inca. (However improbable, it is interesting to note the description of the Chimu set down by Vaca de Castro: according to the Spaniard, the chiefs of the villages were women, and the court lived in incredible luxury and wealth, with dishware of gold and emeralds.) Sarmiento de Gamboa, however, provides a different view of the role played by Viracocha Inca; as is his custom, Sarmiento describes him as cruel and violent, accusing him of having assassinated the old *curaca* Tocay Capac, who had been related to the imperial family. In any case, all agree that the great Viracocha Inca was succeeded by the still greater Cusi Yupanqui, who assumed the name of Pachacuti.

Many ethnologists and Americanists have tried during the last fifty years to explain the meaning of the Pachacuti, the name of the great Inca who governed from 1438 to 1471. According to the old Spanish chroniclers, it meant some variation of "a new way of life," or "reformer of the world." The significance of the two words that make up the name in the Quechua language is known: *pacha* means "land" or "time" and *cuti* means "to turn around." So the theory most generally accepted today is that the name does refer to the "great reform" carried out by this ninth Inca emperor. First and foremost, he is said to have reformed the worship of the Sun, to which were dedicated too many *orejones* — the special class of nobility established by the now large family of the royal Inca. One explanation of the rise of these *orejones* is that the ever-increasing number of imperial concubines gave the emperor a great number of illegitimate offspring. The male children became court officials, or administrators of the cult and of the possessions of the Sun god. They adorned their ears with heavy gold discs, thus explaining the curious name given to them by the Spaniards — *orejones*, or "big-eared ones."

But long before the Spaniards, according to the legend, Pachacuti realized that these priests, with their prophecies and their claims to interpret the will of the ancestor-god, were threatening to restrict the power of the emperor. It was thus necessary to give the Sun, and hence its descendants, an ancestor; this was Pachacamac, the creator of all things. The priests tried to oppose this new overbearing god, but the emperor responded: "The Sun works as well, getting up early in the morning, warming the earth, and retiring in the evening. Who commands it, if not its Lord, the creator of all things, the great Pachacamac?" The theological dispute ended in favor of the emperor. The Inca had a new and more powerful ancestor, but the cult did not spread into the *ayllus*. Pachacamac was a god of Cuzco, mentioned during official ceremonies, but without temples or priests.

There are many other stories that surrounded the great Pachacuti. One was that he was actually the *curaca* of another people who defeated the son of Viracocha Inca and became lord of Cuzco. According to other accounts, Pachacuti was the third of Viracocha Inca's four sons, who because of his courageous exploits took over the Inca empire in place of the first-born, Urcon. This story claimed that two chieftains of the Chanca peoples had rounded up a large band of warriors and were threatening Cuzco. As a banner, they used the mummy of one of their ancestors, the Anco Ayllo who had already caused the Inca such trouble in the southeastern territory. The two rebels had long been raiding lands of the empire, but neither old Viracocha Inca nor Urcon had ever dared to make war against them. Emboldened by the indecision of their adversaries, the followers of Anco Ayllo finally decided to raid Cuzco. Their

The legendary founder of the Inca dynasty, Manco Capac (top), and his sister-wife, Mama Óllo (bottom). These and the other such primitive illustrations that follow are from the seventeenth-century work of Felipe Guaman Poma de Ayala (see page 187).

Right: The Inca emperor sacrificing to the Sun.
A) Sacrifice with offerings of gold and silver
B) Sacrifice with black lamb
C) Sacrifice for the sowing of crops

A

B

C

band had by this time grown to the strength of a full-scale army, and the *orejones* advised the emperor and his heir-apparent to flee, thus leaving Cusi Yupanqui to defend the city, together with his trusted captains.

Rather than waiting for the assault of his enemies, Cusi Yupanqui ordered a sudden sortie, aiming directly at the column carrying the totemic-banner and forcing the superstitious troops to flee. When the marauders were finally defeated, Cusi Yupanqui gathered the insignia of the enemy and sent them to Cuzco so that his father could trample on them, as was the custom. Old Viracocha would have preferred to have this honor reserved for his favorite son, Urcon, but the *orejones* acclaimed Cusi Yupanqui instead with the symbolic name of Pachacuti. So it was that Cusi Yupanqui was named emperor while his father was still alive. As can be seen, the story of Pachacuti's feats and those of his father are quite similar: both defeat the Chancas, one of them wounding Anco Ayllo, the other fighting his mummy.

Pachacuti was not only reputed to be a great warrior but also a man who promoted a series of reforms. He perfected the calendar and the system used in census-taking; he is credited with designing the city of Cuzco; and he transformed the Temple of the Sun into a great Inca sanctuary, a *huaca* for the entire territory. A late exploit of far-reaching importance was his conquest of the kingdom of the Collas, located south of Cuzco in the quarter of the empire known as Collasuyu. The Colla chiefs were taken to Cuzco; their leader, Chuchi Capac, was slain and his remains trampled on in the Temple of the Sun. One hundred sixty leagues of territory, from the coast to the Mojos Mountains, thus fell under the administration of Pachacuti. The Collas, who now became *mitimaes,* were transferred to various localities while their lands were colonized by new inhabitants known to be loyal to the Inca. The sons of Chuchi Capac, who had been obliged to work at Tambo, eight leagues from Cuzco, managed to escape and for the remainder of their lives they fought against the Inca, inciting the Collas to revolt, even after the death of Pachacuti, under the empire of his successor, Topa Yupanqui.

Emperor Topa Yupanqui captured Quito to the north and pushed as far as the Maule River, in what is today Chile, fighting the Diaguitis and the Araucanians. But while he was busy fighting, his brothers in Cuzco were conspiring against him. Topa wisely returned to his homeland and, placing his brothers in command of his troops, sent one of them to the north to watch over the Chancas and the other to the south to fight the indomitable Araucanians. When one dared to return to Cuzco, Topa Yupanqui had him put to death.

When Topa Yupanqui died in 1493, he was succeeded by Huayna Capac. By now Cuzco, which numbered more than two hundred thousand inhabitants, was the seat of a particularly large and idle court. Huayna Capac was truly the prince of decadence, if we are to believe some of the chronicles. Sarmiento de Gamboa says Huayna Capac had seven hundred concubines at his disposal, shut in houses built especially for them. He possessed a sumptuous court and one hundred bodyguards of royal blood. Whenever he went out into the streets of the capital he was carried in a golden litter by eight of his captains. The eleventh of the Inca emperors, he is remembered primarily as a legislator and for his attempts to unify the empire, which had reached its greatest degree of expansion in his reign — an area of about 380,000 square miles (approximately all the Atlantic coast states of the United States). Huayna Capac is also credited with having made the Quechua language mandatory among all subjects of the empire; he also created annual holidays, during which he received the *curacas* from the most remote corners of the empire. The participation of the chiefs of the federated villages and territories in these royal festivals represented, of course, an act of submission to the Inca.

The intrigue and internecine struggles for power soon caused the royal family — which was shut away and apparently raised under a rigidly endogamous regime in Hanan-Cuzco (Upper Cuzco) — to be opposed by the nobility descended from the concubines, or *agras,* residing in Hurin-Cuzco (Lower Cuzco). Huayna Capac sought to solve these problems by broadening the range of privileges, not permitting the young people of

Hurin-Cuzco to marry among themselves, and by restoring a measure of power to those who dedicated themselves to the worship of the Sun.

But by now the great federation was under too many strains; already a second center of royal power was being established at Quito, in Ecuador, the new important city of the empire. Huayna Capac frequently went to Quito, and it was during one of these trips — or so we are told by Father Anello Oliva — that he came to know the daughter of an important *curaca* of the Chinchas. The sovereign, not content with having the young woman, Vayara by name, among his many concubines, had a son by her for whom he felt great affection. Five years before Vayara gave birth to Atahualpa, however, the Emperor had had another boy of his legitimate wife in Cuzco and had given him the name of Huascar. On his deathbed, Huayna Capac, torn by loyalty to both his sons, decided to divide his empire into two kingdoms: one would have Quito as its capital and Atahualpa as its lord; Cuzco would remain the capital of the other kingdom, with Huascar on the throne. Not long before he died, Huayna Capac called in Atahualpa, who had just celebrated his fifteenth birthday, and had him swear to live in peace with his half-brother.

Whether Oliva's account is the true story or not, it is a fact that the Inca empire was threatened by a split after Huayna Capac's death. Huascar, feeling he was backed by tradition and by his rights as legitimate heir, ordered his half-brother Atahualpa to come to Cuzco as an act of submission. But instead of complying with the haughty command of his brother, Atahualpa formed an army of the warlike Coza and Manta peoples of Ecuador, tribes who had already given the Inca much trouble at the time of the Inca expansion into their region, and began marching toward the south. Atahualpa himself settled in Cajamarca, far north of Cuzco, but his capable generals led his army south; after a series of battles, they conquered the forces of Huascar and entered Cuzco, where Huascar surrendered and was imprisoned.

Father Oliva tells us that during the victory celebration at Cajamarca, one of Atahualpa's captains, famous for his powers as a soothsayer, became pensive and sad. Atahualpa asked him why, and the captain, breaking into tears, replied: "My lord, last night I had a presage of a great misfortune. What good can come from having defeated and taken prisoner the descendant of the Inca, becoming master of his treasures, if not long from now you yourself will suffer the same fate? And what is worse, it will not be from the hands of Huascar — from whom, as a brother, you might expect pity — that you will fall: if the stars do not deceive me, this will come about at the hands of ferocious foreigners who will have arrived at our shores from the sea. They will put your army to flight and, in the end, murder you. This is the cause of my grief." Atahualpa grew pale with fear at that grim prophecy, and immediately ordered sacrifices to the Sun to render it propitious. But a short time afterward, word came to him that the Spaniards, bearded and clad in iron, had landed in Peru, on the beach near Tumbez.

This was spring of 1532. By November 16 of the same year, Atahualpa was taken prisoner at Cajamarca by the men of Francisco Pizarro. That same winter, while preparing to pay the ransom the Spaniards had demanded for his half-brother, Huascar was drowned by the courtesans of Cuzco in the Addamarca River: according to the chronicles, the order to kill Huascar had been given by Atahualpa himself, out of fear that his brother might obtain the assistance of the Spaniards in assuming the imperial throne. But after the fabulous ransom had been paid — a roomful of gold, valued about $10,000,000 at today's prices — Atahualpa was accused by the Spanish of stirring up the native population and of various other crimes. The beginnings of the Inca imperial dynasty may be shrouded in myth, but the end is a matter of history: on August 29, 1533, Atahualpa, the last Inca emperor, was garroted to death.

DEATH SONG OF PACHACUTI

I was born like a lily in a garden,
and even so was I raised to manhood;
when the time came, I grew old;
and when I had to die, I withered and expired.

(Collected by Pedro Sarmiento, 1572)

TO THE EMPEROR

Fear not, Lord, feel not faint,
  we shall accompany thee and together we
  shall arrive.
We dry thy tears,
  so that thou mayest inhale the scent of
  flowers.
Let us rejoice, let us rejoice.

INCA HYMN OF TARMA

Organization of the Inca State

The penitence and fasting of the emperor and all the people.

There is no proof, from an archaeological point of view, that the structure of Cuzco and the empire responded to the detailed descriptions of the chroniclers, particularly those given by Garcilaso de la Vega, who attributed the origins to the time of Manco Capac. If anything, modern students of the Inca tend to consider Cuzco and the imperial structure as having begun with the Emperor Pachacuti. But whichever Supreme Inca, or *Sapa Inca,* initiated the basic structures, he was building on a solid and deep-rooted foundation. To begin with, there was nature itself, which had made it all but impossible for the *ayllus* to develop beyond their local confines: the traditional village society was not able to look beyond its walls or valley and to think in terms of building roads or providing storehouses for famines. Meanwhile, this same nature that had favored the rural settlements in river valleys had laid out the larger boundaries for a people who, if they remained unacquainted with the wheel, were able to develop elaborate statistical methods for controlling everything that fell within their domain.

The early chroniclers, in fact, laid considerable stress on the meticulous order that seemed so extraordinary to the Spanish conquistadors. This order became the utopian model for Europeans at the very time that the feudal vision of their world was collapsing. The Spaniards, for instance, were surprised not to find a vast class of slaves, and they sought analogies in the Arab civilization, inclined as they were to dividing the world into Christians and "pagans." Later, German geographers and French naturalists sought to establish parallels to Greek and Roman cultures in the Andean agricultural society. It was not by chance that so much speculation was to be found in the book *Historia del Mondo Nuovo* of the Venetian Gerolamo Benzoni, printed in 1565. The Italian was influenced, actually, by the accounts of travelers who had returned from Asia, where the long survival of farming communities, the ownership of water sources, and the generalized slavery made up the socioeconomic patterns that Wittfogel was later to characterize as "Asian despotism."

The emperor making a ceremonial toast to the Sun.

Quite aside from such later interpretations, the extraordinary power of the Inca emperor and the rigid organization of the structures of this power found confirmation in the reliable descriptions made by the Pizarro brothers and by their secretary Francisco de Jerez. When Hernando Pizarro and deSoto visited Atahualpa near Cajamarca, they found him living in a house with a vast courtyard and a series of arcades around a garden. The building was covered with a plaster described as "resplendent" by some and merely as "red and white" by others. In front was a well that supplied hot and cold water for a gigantic swimming pool of square stones, still known today as "the Inca's pool." Atahualpa was at the center of the courtyard surrounded by his courtesans. Simply dressed, he was seated on a low stool and was wearing on his head the *maskapaicha,* or crimson fringe, that was the insignia of Inca sovereignty, used by Atahualpa after his victory over his brother Huascar.

When Atahualpa repaid the visit to the Spaniards, he was carried on a golden palanquin lined with gaily colored feathers and preceded by a swarm of servants who swept the road in front of him. The retinue was made up of hundreds of dignitaries, their ears adorned with gold discs. These were the *orejones,* and as they relieved each other from carrying the heavy sedan-chair of the emperor, the Spanish killed them one by one until Atahualpa was taken prisoner by Pizarro himself. Such lively descriptions, for all their cruelty, reveal the Inca court in all its splendor. When Pizarro's men arrived at Cuzco, of course, Huascar had already been killed; the Spaniards were received by Manco, a younger brother of Huascar (or, some say, a grandson of Huayna Capac). The official Spanish domination of Peru began when the conquistadors placed Manco on the throne: although Manco later attempted to lead a revolt, the Inca empire was at its end.

Celebrations for the festival of the Emperor and the Sun

Standing on a palanquin carried by his subjects, the emperor heads for battle.

The city and the empire that the Spanish took over had probably already moved beyond the "classic" Inca phase, and the descriptions of the chroniclers cannot be considered as true for the entire duration of Inca society. Huascar's court, for instance, had been exterminated by Atahualpa's army, and the Spanish found a Cuzco largely inhabited by relatives and descendants of the emperors and their concubines, a population almost entirely engaged in the administration of religion, the empire, and the army. Highly respected still, however, were the *amautas*, the sages who handled the education of youths of royal blood; these *amautas* also acted as court historians and advisors to the emperors on religious questions.

By the time of the Spanish Conquest, the most important officials of the empire were the *tucricucs*. They administered the far-flung lands of the Emperor and they were always consulted before public works were undertaken. A *tucricuc* traveled a great deal, and he served as link between the imperial court and the *curacas*, who, ever since they had been assigned land, animals, and concubines of their own, had become extremely dependent on the court. When a *tucricuc* visited the *curacas*, he was often accompanied by the *quipucamayoc*, the reader of the *quipu*, who served as a combination accountant-secretary; the *quipucamayoc* thus became responsible for supervising the taxation system as well as the census-taking. The statistical methods used were based on a decimal system and were related to the very organization of the empire.

Life in the villages became somewhat different under the Inca empire, because the *curacas* became both more important yet less meaningful to the villagers. The *curaca* continued to preside over the meetings of the heads of families and still enjoyed a certain prestige, as in the old *ayllus;* but everyone knew that he now derived his authority from the emperor, not from the community. Still, the basic *ayllu* persisted. Don Antonio de Ulloa, writing many years after the Conquest about the Spanish colonial empire in Peru, could say: "Even after so many years . . . it is impossible to make this nation set aside its old customs and usages, and if we were to try to do so it would be even worse, because if the people here were forbidden to hold their junta meetings publicly they would meet at night in secluded places where it would be impossible to control what was being said." In the end, the Viceroy of Charles the Fifth had to preserve the communities and place them at his empire's service, just as the Inca had done when assembling their empire.

The inhabitants of the *ayllu* were subdivided for statistical purposes into ten or twelve categories; the latter were outlined by Diego de Ortega Morejon and Cristobal de Castro in a report dated 1558 as follows:

1. One to three months: *antaguamarca* ("sleeping child")
2. Four to eight months: *sompeguamarca* ("child in swaddling clothes")
3. Eight months to one year: *traguamarca* ("defenseless child")
4. One to two years: *lloca* ("child that moves on all fours")
5. Two to four years: *machapora* ("child easily frightened")
6. Four to eight years: *tarariquea* ("child not yet separated from parents")
7. Eight to twelve years: *guamarca* ("child")
8. Twelve to sixteen years: *cocopallac* ("gatherer of coca")
9. Sixteen to twenty years: *michoguayna* (probably "messenger" or "runner")
10. Twenty to forty years: *avcapora* ("warrior")
11. Forty to sixty years: *chavpilco* ("middle-aged man")
12. Sixty years and over: *punoloco* ("old sleepyhead")

If there seems to be a strong bias toward the boys and men in Inca society, this impression is quite true. This was especially evident in the custom of separating young girls about the age of ten into two groups. By far the larger number were left in the villages, where they were married

Sacsahuamán: The three sawtooth walls, one within and above the other, that make up the fortress.

off to become wives and mothers and to perform the domestic and agricultural chores. But the government officials who periodically visited the villages would select those that appeared most physically perfect and send them to provincial capitals where they spent the next four years being trained in such things as weaving, cooking, religious practices, etc. These girls were known as the *acclacunas*, the "Chosen Women" — and perhaps the greatest honor of all was to be further singled out to be sacrificed on special occasions. Those who survived the years of training were divided again. Some were given as secondary wives to nobles or even presented to the emperor himself as concubines. The rest were sworn to chastity and consecrated to serve in the shrines, where they prepared the *chicha* drink or wove fabrics. These latter lived in conventlike institutions, presided over by priestesses of noble birth, and it is this group that became known as the "Virgins of the Sun." Even the girls of royal blood were raised for lives of service to the court and they accepted that they would be married off to the proper officials. And any girl in the empire might find herself taken as a concubine by the emperor or as a servant for the imperial court.

The two Spanish chroniclers who reported on the twelve categories for the census described the actual census-taking as follows:

"On entering a valley, the envoy of the emperor, known as a *runaquipa*, would gather together all commoners and upper-class people, divided into *guarangas* (groups of one thousand), *pachacas* (groups of one hundred), and *chungas* (groups of ten). Then he would have them sit on the ground, even if they were near to dying, and count them, dividing them up into the twelve age groups. Since there would always be changes compared to the preceding census, he would select a few new *yanaconas* [for the imperial work-force] who looked best to him; he would also choose the girls who would serve the emperor and the Sun, as he had been commanded to do. And if he saw that the population was increasing, to the extent that a new chief of a *guaranga*, a *pachaca*, or a *chunga*, could be named, he would record this on his *quipu* and report the fact to the emperor so that as the people reached a certain number, new chiefs might be named."

The *runaquipa* was also authorized to mete out punishment — using a whip with a stone tied to its end — for certain types of crime, but the main judicial officials of the Inca empire were the *ochacamayocs*, appointed from among the illegitimate descendants of the emperor. They, too, paid periodic visits to the territory of the confederation, administering justice as they saw fit, applying the laws (which were, of course, unwritten), and handing down punishments to suit whatever crimes were brought to their attention. Crimes might include everything from errors in calculating the amount of tribute owed to the Emperor to the more obvious crime of murder. The law was especially hard on any commoners who presumed to have sexual relations with a woman assigned to the nobility or the emperor's court.

Undoubtedly, though, the subdividing into groups and the whole system of keeping track of the people was primarily aimed at obtaining men for the *mita* — the compulsory service in the imperial army or for great public works such as aqueducts, roads, or agricultural terraces. This was a form of taxation, really, that all commoners had to expect to pay at some time or another. But the control of the population was also necessary for the Inca to maintain two rather special groups within the Inca empire — the *mitimaes* and the *yanaconas*, both of which we have referred to in passing. The *mitimaes* were the groups of people — whole *ayllus* and possibly larger groups — transferred about to colonize or to pacify regions. There is some question as to when the Inca instituted this practice; certainly it was used in the late phase of the empire, particularly against the Collas in the south, who were always resisting the Inca authority.

The *yanaconas*, meanwhile, were the class of servants (in the Quechua language, *yanay* means "to serve"), used especially at Cuzco and in its environs to build temples, bridges and roads, to work in the mines, to cultivate the royal fields, and to perform menial tasks in the capital. According to some scholars, the *yanaconas* were also used at the court of

As soon as the Inca had made themselves lords of a province, they caused the natives, who had previously been widely scattered, to live in communities, with an officer over every ten, another over every hundred, another over every thousand, another over every ten thousand, and an Inca governor over all, who reported upon the administration every year, recording the births and the deaths that had occurred among men and flocks, the yield of the crops, and all other details, with great minuteness. They left Cuzco every year, and returned in February, to make their report, before the festival of Raimi began, bringing with them the tribute of the whole empire. This system was advantageous and good, and it was most important in maintaining the authority of the Inca. Every governor, no matter how great a lord he might be, entered Cuzco with a burden on his back. This was a ceremony that was never dispensed with, and it gave great authority to the Inca Emperors.

POLO DE ONDEGARDO: *Report* (c. 1560).

Sacsahuamán: The foundation of the circular tower on the level clearing at the very top of the fortress; this served as the residence of the emperor when he spent any time here.

Cuzco: The famous "stone of the twelve angles" in a wall of the late Inca period. Whatever possessed the designer of such an element, the work was achieved with great refinement.

the emperor as administrators and bodyguards. Although at first the *yanaconas* were a quite separate and self-reproducing group, in the later phase of the empire they were also being taken from local communities. "By depriving the communities of some of their members," writes Alfred Metraux, "the Inca weakened them and laid the groundwork for a revolution that, if there had been enough time, might have changed the structure of the empire. From a group of largely autonomous rural communities, the Inca might have created a sort of "pre-feudal" empire, in which noblemen and officials would have possessed great dominions, worked by serfs and even by slaves."

Whether the *yanaconas* should be thought of as "slaves" is perhaps academic, given the virtually absolute necessity of nearly everyone under Inca rule to accept his lot in life. One authority, Louis Baudin, has said: "It was a full-fledged slavery, to which they had to submit, along with their descendants, as long as they lived, since they were, so to speak, excluded from society." Another modern authority, Luis Valcárcel, stresses more the fact that they were social pariahs, the *huaca*-less — that is, those without a sacred shrine of their own, removed from any *ayllu*.

Valcárcel goes on to claim that "at the time of the Conquest, they [the *yanaconas*] were the natural allies of the conquistadors; they were the fifth column, the inside collaborators of the Spanish invaders, fighting against their own brothers." This may be a bit extreme, but there is no denying that the *mitimaes* and the *yanaconas* help to explain the mild reaction of so many of the Andean natives to the Spanish invaders: such people would prefer to support the defeat of the Inca by almost anyone — not realizing, of course, that the foreigners would soon become lords who took over all the Inca privileges and more.

Saihuite: The natural stone has been sculptured with elements that probably represent a model of a mountain sanctuary, much like that of the Kenko stone (page 167).

Finally, though, it must be borne in mind that this phenomenon — the existence of the *mitimaes* and the *yanaconas* — occurred within a society where there was a balance of forces, if only a primitive one, between the imperial court, its priests, and its noblemen on the one hand, and the peasant communities with their *curacas* on the other. This balance of forces, along with such facts that there were no large landed estates as such, or that the building techniques required only local natural resources, created these distinctive social groups. Call them forms of slavery or otherwise, but it should also be said that the Inca mythology helped to create a slave who would be happy to serve a more or less direct descendant of the Sun.

Cuzco: The Center of the World

Perhaps the best way to approach the Inca capital is through the eyes of some of the early chroniclers — realizing, as usual, that they are transmitting a fair amount of legend along with history. Garcilaso de la Vega described Cuzco as follows:

"The ancient Inca kings divided Cuzco into quarters resembling the four parts of their empire, which they called *Tahuantinsuyu*. This occurred at the very outset, at the time of the first king, Manco Capac. He ordered that the wild populations he had conquered should people the city in keeping with the regions of their origins. Thus, the peoples he subjected in the east were to inhabit the eastern part of the city; those of the west, the western part; the same was true for the peoples of the north and the south. As a result, the initial inhabitants of Cuzco were spread out in an immense circle around the center of Inca power. Each cardinal point corresponded, therefore, both with the direction of the country from which the immigrant had come and with the part of the city in which he had taken up residence. The *curacas* built themselves homes (where they stayed when they had to come to court) in districts corresponding to the geographical position of their provinces; those from the north, in the north; those from the south, in the south; and so on. And the house of each *curaca* was surrounded by the houses of his subjects. So it was that in walking through the various neighborhoods one was visiting the entire empire, as represented by its provinces, its inhabitants, and its customs. One could rightly say that Cuzco was the portrait and microcosm of the entire empire. As a result, the peoples who had been subjected from one end of the empire to the other lived only in the outermost ring of the city (where neither the Inca emperors nor even their families or relatives ever took up residence), grouped together in extramural quarters, outside the city proper."

After reading Garcilaso's account of this perfectly planned city of Cuzco, it might seem a contradiction to know that it was oriented toward the cardinal points in a rather special manner: the axes of the city formed an angle of forty-five degrees with the astronomical directions. The reasons behind this design — which can hardly be considered accidental — involve two types of problems. The first, which we might characterize as of a theoretical nature, departs from the interpretation of the cross as a static pattern and conceives of it as a dynamic one. If the cross oriented toward the cardinal points indicates the expansion of the center without implicating movement, a cross superimposed over it at a forty-five-degree angle indicates the most hidden principle of rotary motion, and hence the passing of time. This is a widespread symbolism that was already present in the well-known solar "swastikas" of Euro-Asian prehistory; it is also accepted that the symbolism of the cross is linked to the solar pictograph. Closer to Inca culture, we may cite the example of the Mesoamerican hieroglyph symbolic of movement — a diagonal cross or similar figures. It is through movement, then, that the structure of the city is rendered explicit, a structure in which a shifting of inhabitants from the center to the outskirts throws light on the hierarchy between the central point and the peripheral points; the circular movement shows the topographical and territorial relationships of the various populations of

the empire. Like a compass card whose main axes are understood, the choice of the intermediate axes is believed to have permitted the division of the circle into eight sectors.

The eight-sector radial structure, which among other things is a widespread solar symbol, was frequently to be found in the typology of individual buildings in Cuzco. The most fitting instance is the main tower of the Sacsahuamán fortress, above Cuzco; this tower may be considered the most stable link between the material structure of the capital city, its mythical origins, and the celestial regions of space. It was probably through this tower that the mystical tie between the Inca emperor and the heavens was perpetuated. Clearly expressed in it was the principle of the vertical axis and of radiation in the various horizontal regions of space.

The second problem in reconciling the layout of Cuzco with its ideology involves the territory of which the city wanted to consider itself not only the ideal but also the true geometric center. If, as seems to be the case, the final structure of the capital was a late reconstruction — a period when the "four quarters" of the empire had already been well defined — the orientation of Cuzco appears to be a logical consequence of its geographical position. Consider the place of origin that one of the oldest legends assigned to the Inca stock: Lake Titicaca. Both the Island of the Sun (in that lake) and Tiahuanaco (nearby) come close to being located on the prolongation of the main axis of Cuzco — the axis running northwest-southeast. This direction therefore also represents the spatial and temporal dependence of the Inca on the Titicaca "cradle" of their civilization.

This same axis, extended to a point northwest of Cuzco, encounters Chavín de Huantar, marking out a sort of spinal column approximately parallel to the Andean chain, but clearly based on territorial relationships produced by a long evolution of the various Andean political centers. This ideal axis runs virtually parallel to the coast in its southern stretch, and it is therefore in harmony with the needs of a natural coordination between Cuzco and the surrounding territory.

In this resolution of the apparent inconsistencies in the orientation of Cuzco's layout, we may perceive a trait typical of the eminently practical character of Inca "science": it never ran counter to nature, but always strove to extract intelligent interpretations of whatever nature itself suggested. It is evident, in fact, that the harmony between capital and kingdom, far from being an abstract assumption of principle, became a dynamic motive of integration, valid even beyond the initial planning of the city. The precise geometry dominating the urban and artistic concepts of the preceding Andean cultures gave way under the Inca to a more universal interpretation of the eternal relationships between the achievements of man and the conditionings of nature.

The celebration of the founding of Cuzco, for instance, coincided with the festival devoted to the advent of spring. The various ceremonies revealed the meaning of the division of the city and the Inca state into four parts. The Emperor issued forth from the Sacsahuamán fortress at dawn, clad in the garments of a messenger of the Sun, carrying in his right hand the golden lance that was the symbol of command and the highest insignia of the Inca army. The emperor descended the slope at a run, arriving at the main square where he was awaited by four princes of the royal blood brandishing lances and ready for the race. As the messenger of the Sun, the emperor ordered them to start out immediately and to drive all evils from the confines of the city — and therefore symbolically from the entire Inca world. All four set out at a run, each taking one of the roads leading to the four parts of the Tahuantinsuyu. After a quarter of a league, these messengers of royal birth passed the lances to another four, and so on, until some six leagues had been covered in relays. Then the lances were thrust into the ground and the evils driven away; it was thought that they were swallowed up either by a river or by a precipice.

The meaning of this festival is clear with regard to the spatial symbolism of the tie between the sacred center and the four axes of expansion of the beneficial divine principle. But it is also interesting to connect the race of these ninety-six royal *chasquis*, armed with lances and running off into the four cardinal directions, with the ritual race of the forty-eight (exactly half) royal messengers we encountered at Tiahuanaco. And this is only one of the more striking parallelisms demonstrating the relationship of the Inca civilization with the culture of Lake Titicaca.

Cuzco (which in the Quechua language means "navel") arose therefore in the center of the entire empire, marking the exact point where the golden staff of Manco Capac had sunk into the ground. This was the point where the power contact between divinity and man was favorable, guaranteeing both the propitious position of the "navel" of the world and its long temporal duration. An imaginary vertical axis, an *intihuatana* (or solar observatory) marking the contact with the Sun, was perhaps represented by the main tower of the capital's fortress, Sacsahuamán. The sacred center of Cuzco constituted the point of departure for all operations aimed at the measurement of space, concentrating in itself as it did the maximum of sacredness.

At the center of the system of *ceques* (a kind of modular system), Cuzco determined the position and relative importance of all the other sacred localities of the empire; as the gathering knot of a gigantic, imaginary *quipu*, it served to bring together in one system all the spatial subdivisions and temporal successions of the Inca people. This unique sacred city reflected in a fundamentally perfect model the entire organization of the empire, of which it was a sort of mnemonic pattern, a table for immediate consultation. Successive viewings would extract from the ideal shape of the city not only the structure of the state at large but also its hierarchical functioning — perhaps even the chronological succession of the emperors. One might even recognize a concept of the city that is literally anthropomorphic (e.g., a navel, a head, arms); but the "navel" was primarily geometrical, in that it made it possible to orient all calculations and mathematical operations involving the entire state structure.

The pointed center from which the main directions of the state radiate is a concept that was also to be found in the other pre-Inca cities, at first used for magical-religious ends, and then ever more openly for administrative purposes. The single center was first and foremost the symbol of the absolute, autocratic power of one sole lord: the symbol of the Sun had not been chosen by chance, but corresponded exactly to the radiation from one sole point of the beneficial power of the emperor. Cuzco, seen in this way, was a solar disc placed at the center of the immense Inca territory, a center from which power radiated through the hierarchy of directions.

The division of the city of Cuzco into two halves — situated in keeping with the precise hierarchy but substantially complementary and equal — has been correctly interpreted as an extension to the sacred capital of a social organization to be found in the *ayllus* (and traces of which are noticeable to this day in several ethnic groups in South America). It is probable, moreover, that following the subdivision of Cuzco by Manco Capac into an "upper" part, Hanan-Cuzco (set aside for the emperor's followers) and a "lower" part, Hurin-Cuzco (for those who were attached to his sister-wife, Coya), the custom was codified and extended to the other major cities of the empire. Among those who take this view was Garcilaso, who attributed to these halves a special division, identifying the rich with the Hanansuyu quarter and the poor with the Hurinsuyu quarter. In Cuzco, the demarcation line ran from northeast to southwest, coinciding with the road that cut through the Andes mountains at right angles and therefore separated the entire northern part of the empire from the southern part.

From a more strict viewpoint of urban design, the basic structure of Cuzco was based on four roads, the four arms of a cross, whose center was situated in the main square, ideally in the Temple of the Sun. The empire had been given the highly significant name of Tahuantinsuyu ("the joining of the four parts"), in reference both to the structure of the sacred city itself and to the structure of the cosmos on which it was based. The four *suyus*, or regions into which the immense territory had been

"The first settlement in this valley," continued my uncle the Inca, "was made on the hill called Huanacauti, to the south of the city. It was here that the scepter of gold buried itself in the ground with great ease, and it was never seen again. Then our Emperor said to his wife and sister: 'Our Father the Sun orders that we settle in this valley to fulfill his wishes. It is therefore right, O queen and sister, that each of us should gather these people together, to instruct them and to do the good that has been ordered by our Father the Sun.' Our first rulers set out from the hill of Huanacauti, in different directions, to call the people together, and as this is the first place we know of which they pressed with their feet, we have built a temple here, as is well known, wherein to worship our Father the Sun, in memory of this act of benevolence which He performed for the world."

GARCILASO DE LA VEGA: *Comentarios
Reales* (1609)

divided, had the center of Cuzco in common, for this is where the four roads that linked them to the center of the empire had their beginning. And since the city was oriented not to the cardinal points, as we saw, but to the intermediate directions, each road led, ideally speaking, precisely to the center of each region. The four regions were: to the west, the *Contisuyu*, the sector on the south coast, reached by the road leading southwest; to the south, the *Collasuyu*, the land of the Collas, the high plateau of Lake Titicaca, reached by the road leading southeast; to the east, the *Antisuyu*, the eastern sector, reached by the road leading northeast; and to the north, the *Chinchasuyu*, the northern sector of the coast and the highlands as far as Quito, reached by the road leading northwest.

This layout of Cuzco is attributed by tradition to the great Inca emperor, Pachacuti, who, in conquering the territory of the Chancas to the north and the Collas to the south, had also laid the territorial basis for the great Inca empire. Pachacuti is believed not only to have organized the city but also to have planned the building of the Sacsahuamán fortress. Other sectors of the kingdom were added later by Topo Yupanqui (with the Chimu realm and the southern regions in Chilean territory) and by Huayna Capac (who extended the empire as far as Colombia).

It is interesting to note how, aside from this last undertaking, the conquests of Pachacuti and Topo Yupanqui appeared to answer the need of balancing the new territories around the capital. It would seem that, to accord with events handed down in the legends, these extensions of the empire took place in such a way as to keep Cuzco more or less in the precise center of the empire. This evidently resulted from a carefully devised program of radial expansion, which not only protected the capital but guaranteed its constant commercial supremacy, owing to its dominant central position as a crossroads. The two phases of expansion occurred, furthermore, along the longitudinal axis of the Andean range in symmetry with the transversal axis that passed through Cuzco, linking the mountains to the sea.

The Temple of the Sun

The ideal center of the empire, situated where the four roads came together, was the *Coricancha* ("place of gold"), traditionally known as the Temple of the Sun, although there is some question whether the temple was not primarily dedicated to Viracocha, the creator of all things. This sanctuary (on whose remains the mother church of the Spanish Dominicans was erected) occupied a vast area; evidently it was mainly one large hall, with smaller chapels around it, but there is much disagreement about the details of this temple. All religious events throughout the Inca empire took this Temple of the Sun as a point of reference; each and every sanctuary throughout the empire was built in imitation of this central sanctuary. It was not only the radial point of the four roads of Tahuantinsuyu but also the ideal origin of all the other intermediate directions of space, grouped together in accordance with various geometric subdivisions and in answer to the needs of a "perfect" representation of society. The *huacas* situated around the city, or inside it, all faced the Temple of the Sun, and were located by means of a system of polar coordinates. This ideal radiation, which involved more than five hundred sacred places in the capital areas alone, conformed with the capital's fundamental structure, and this structure in turn was determined by the social structure.

Each one of the *huacas* belonged to a given sector (upper or lower) of the city, and at the same time to one of its quarters. This was part of the system of *ceques*, which on the whole may be said to have represented the fundamental pattern of Inca spatial organization. The authority, R. T. Zuidema, has suggested that this *ceque* system is the most effective key to understanding the organization of Cuzco, and therefore of the entire Inca empire, from both the anthropological and historical viewpoint. In fact, the highly complex model that, with a few variants, served as spatial

Tambo Colorado: A close-up of a wall shows how the *adobe* and *tapia* were evidently used to imitate the stone structures found in the highlands.

representation of phenomena that could not be represented through social relations (e.g., the historical succession of the Inca emperors, the relationships among the *ayllus* and among the groups making up each one of them) must be considered previous even to its partial application in the structure of the capital. It can unquestionably be traced back to an elaboration of relationships between space and time, between unity and multiplicity, between the achievements of man and the cosmos, which prior to the Inca civilization had attained at least a mystical-theological definition.

The Temple of the Sun, as mentioned, seems to have been made up of a number of structures built around a sacred enclosure, and the smaller units were consecrated to other deities. Garcilaso de la Vega once again provides a colorful description of the temple, although it is of uncertain reliability:

"The entire temple was built of large, flat stones, painstakingly shaped and dressed. . . . This most sacred place faced the east. The roof on that side was very high, in order to permit air to circulate, thus keeping the altar clean. Perhaps because there had been no time to put together a more suitable kind of covering, the roof had been thatched with straw, the best that could be found. All the walls were covered from top to bottom by thick plates of pure gold. Emblazoned on the main wall was a likeness of the Sun god, entirely fashioned out of laminated gold. The holy likeness was round in shape and had been made like a human countenance radiating rays of light and flames. . . . Placed to the left and right of the image of the Sun were the mummies of the Inca emperors, arranged according to their antiquity; to look at them one would have thought they were alive. They were all seated on thrones of gold, which were in turn supported by golden pedestals. . . .

"As soon as one entered, one found oneself in a courtyard surrounded by four walls, one of which was part of the main wall of the temple itself. Running around the entire space at the upper limit of the courtyard was a two-palms wide molding of the purest gold, enclosing it like a golden crown. . . . Opening out on the four sides of the cloister were five gigantic square chapels, each one distinctly separated from the others. The roof of these five chapels rose up in the form of a pyramid. The first chapel

Tambo Colorado: A series of chambers with trapezoidal doors and windows, and with many of the walls still bearing traces of the painted plaster.

was consecrated to the Moon, sister and wife of the Sun and for this reason closest to the place where the Sun was worshiped. Everything in this chapel was made of purest silver: the outer walls, the roof, the doors, the inner walls, so that from the bright splendor of the silver everyone could realize he was in the Temple of the Moon. . . . On either side of the image of the Moon (a round countenance of a woman, fashioned of silver) lay the embalmed remains of the queens. . . .

"Another one of the five chapels — to be exact, the one nearest to the sanctuary of the Moon — was consecrated to the star Venus; it was also consecrated to the Pleiades and to the infinite host of other stars that roam the heavens. . . . This chapel, which we may call the stellar chamber, was entirely lined with silver, like that of the Moon. Small golden stars, such as those to be seen in the sky at night, were represented in the ceiling.

"The third chapel, which was next to that of the Moon, was consecrated to the veneration of the Thunder and the Lightning, which in the Inca language were grouped under one term, *Illapa*. . . . The fourth chapel had been consecrated to the Rainbow. This chapel was completely lined with the purest gold. Painted on an enormous arch that spanned the walls of the edifice was the rainbow, with its seven changing hues and all its beauty. The Rainbow, known as the *Chuychu*, was devoutly venerated. . . . The fifth and last chamber of the temple was set aside for the high priests and also the minor priests called upon to officiate in the service of the temple. This chapel, like the other four, was lined from top to bottom with gold, silver, and precious stones. . . ."

The great *Coricancha*, together with the area of the royal residence, was the holiest part of the monumental center of Cuzco. The area of the city where the most ancient royal palace had been built was situated in Hanan-Cuzco, on the slope leading up to the Sacsahuamán fortress, and was called *Colcampata;* it is believed to be the place where the palace of the founder of the dynasty and of the city of Cuzco, Manco Capac, had been located. Prominent among the other sacred complexes in the center of Cuzco was the Acclahuasi, the "convent" of the Virgins of the Sun. According to Cristobal de Molina, there were four thousand people assigned to the various sacred functions within the capital.

Around the central area of Cuzco were the dwellings of the former Inca sovereigns: tradition claimed that each king had built himself a new palace. Then, in the next "ring" were the *canchas,* or enclosures, each inhabited by an *ayllu*. Still farther out were the lodgings used by the *curacas* when they came to pay their respects to the emperor. And still farther out was a peripheral ribbon of humble dwellings for the commoners, organized in *ayllus:* this band was considered external to the sacred confines of the city. The sacred nature of Cuzco was further revealed by the petty customs recorded by the chroniclers, such as the story that those who were coming into the city would step aside for those who were leaving it: the latter were already invested to some degree with the holiness of the place. But it was during the four annual festivals, which coincided with the solstices, when the *curacas* came in from all corners of the empire to pay homage to the Sun and the emperor, taking part in complicated propitiatory ceremonies, that Cuzco must have truly blended all its many elements into a living sacred community.

Sacsahuamán

The sense of absolute domination of the emperor and his kindred over Cuzco and the surrounding territory was effectively expressed in the gigantic defensive complex overlooking the city. The fortress, known as Sacsahuamán (which literally meant "imperial falcon"), also represented the geographical origins of the city, for according to Garcilaso, the first settlement of Manco Capac rose on this very hill. It was also the heights of this hill that contained the source of the stream that cut longitudinally through Cuzco, dividing the city proper from the suburbs, and turning

A functionary of the emperor visiting the territory under his jurisdiction.

A chasqui, *or courier, running along the road; in his left hand he carries a* quipu, *a knotted cord with a record of some numbers, while he takes a drink from a vessel in his right hand.*

Pachacamac: A close-up of a section of the
Temple of the Sun, which the Inca built to
dominate an earlier and celebrated Andean
sanctuary.

southeast, marked the direction of the great road to the Collasuyu. At the opposite end of Sacsahuamán the stream cut through the last (that is, the lowest) quarter of Cuzco, known as Pumachupan, "the puma's tail." At right angles to the stream ran the road that divided Cuzco into two parts. The fortress therefore was the veritable "head" of Cuzco, in that it crowned the uppermost part. Again, there is the suggestion of an anthropomorphic symbolism, with the "tail" of the organism situated at the other extremity, the furthermost point of the lowest section of the city.

The main fortress was said to have been planned by Pachacuti and the work begun under Topa Yupanqui, but although the work continued for more than fifty years, it was not yet completed by the time the Spaniards arrived. Three walls, erected on terraces and built of enormous stones, formed a powerful defensive barrier that faced out over Cuzco; on the opposite side, a simple wall closed in the fortress, for it sat along the edge of a natural precipice. The three walls or ramparts have a total height of sixty feet; the outside, or lowest, one reveals the most accurate building techniques as well as the largest stone blocks. (One of these stones is twenty feet high, ten feet wide, and nine feet thick.) Three doorways opened through this lowest wall, but all were easily defended. Inside each of the three walls was a trenchlike gallery for the guards to make their rounds in (similar to the one at Paramonga).

The design of the three defense lines complied with a particular strategy, based on the sawtoothed contour of the walls. This produced a series of corners that protruded, and others at the recessions. The main purpose appears to have been to increase the effectiveness of the lateral protection or flanking operations against frontal assaults. Each jutting corner dominated two stretches of wall, thus making it possible to get at assailants of the next bastion both from behind and from the side.

The uppermost area of the fortress was a triangular clearing closed in by three towers that protected its highest points. The main tower, the *Moyoc-marca* ("round fortress"), was round and had an internal structure based on eight radial sectors. It also included a spring and served as the residence of the emperor when he came to Sacsahuamán; it was even equipped to house his principal court. The other two towers, square in shape, served as quarters for the garrison. An intricate network of tunnels and underground passageways lined with stone ran beneath the citadel, linking the three towers and forming a sort of labyrinth at least as complex as the structure above ground. For all this, it is generally agreed that this impressive fortress was never needed or used in any military action: it was essentially a show of strength by the Inca emperors and if it was to be used, it would probably serve as a refuge place for the emperor and his court.

Roads, Tambos, and Forts

Perhaps the most striking instrument of governmental control employed by the Inca, and one bound up with the concept of the unified state, was the celebrated network of roads. They made a great impression on the Spanish conquistadors and the chroniclers; and some of them have been incorporated into the Peruvian highway system of today. The best description that has come down to us is that of Cieza de Leon, who focused his attention on the main artery, or "royal highway," the longitudinal route along the highlands of the Andes.

"The Inca built the longest and most important road in the world, which ran from Cuzco to Quito and, at one time, from Cuzco to Chile, covering a distance of eight hundred leagues. I do not think anything so grandiose as to equal this road has been built in all human history. It crosses deep valleys and the highest mountains, passing snowy peaks and waterfalls, cutting through solid rock and skirting tortuous mountain torrents. In all of these places the road is solidly built, held up by terracing along the slopes. It is cut into the rock along the banks of rivers and protected by supporting walls. At the snowy summits it is provided with steps and benches where travelers can catch their breath, and for its

REGIDORES
TENGA·LIBRO·QVÍPO·CV

CÕTADOR·MAIOR·ITEZORERO
TAVANTINSVIOQVÍPOC
CVRACA·CON ❦ DOR·CHAVA

Functionaries of the emperor
A) A tucricuc, an administrator of a large province
B) An inspector of the roads
C) An inspector of bridges
D) A quipucamayoc, a "reader of the quipu," in charge of the census and taxation
E) An accountant-treasurer, with a quipu in his hands and an abacus-type device in the corner

entire length it is kept open and clear of rubble at all times. Placed at regular intervals are resting places, storehouses with provisions, and Sun temples."

The Inca network of roads was made up of two major longitudinal routes — the one through the highlands and a parallel road along the coast — with a number of roads also connecting the various centers along the coast; it was the first time that some of these ancient cities were linked in this way. Numerous transversal roads from the coast to the highlands facilitated trade, especially in the food and products characteristic of the two areas, but it was as a communication system that these roads were most crucial.

The swiftness of the communication system depended on the couriers, the *chasquis,* who could move messages or small goods between Cuzco and the coast in about two days (thus keeping the emperor supplied with fresh fish!). The speed with which such distances were covered was due to the great numbers of *chasquis,* who relieved each other about every mile — the distance a healthy young man was expected to be able to run. The *chasquis* awaited the arrival of their fellow couriers in way-stations, and went out to meet them to speed up the transfer of a message in this long "relay race" against time. The system allowed the emperor to receive the most important reports in a surprisingly short time: messages arrived from Pachacamac in Cuzco in three days, from Quito in five days.

Another use for the roads, although one reserved almost exclusively for the imperial government, was the transportation by llama-trains of products such as vicuña woolens, coconuts, *chicha* (the maize beer), and other items prized by the court at Cuzco. The roads, then, were designed for the transit of human beings and llamas, not for wheeled vehicles, although they were, in fact, paved along many stretches. But in the most difficult terrain the road became little more than a path, often with steps, which made it possible to move along only in single file. Along the flat land, and especially in the vicinity of the main cities, the roads widened out to twelve to fifteen feet, so that many persons or llamas could pass at the same time. This was important because chief among the roads' primary purposes was that of moving the imperial armies on their various military expeditions — and the royal family on inspection trips or pleasure excursions. Later the roads were used by Pizarro and his men to race from one part of the hostile kingdom to the other on horseback: one of the causes of the rapid disintegration of the Inca resistance was due to the ease with which the Spanish horsemen could move around on these very convenient roads.

To provide lodgings and refreshments for people traveling on official business, an elaborate network of rest-houses, the *tambos,* was set up at more or less constant intervals. The basic *tambo* was about one day's journey from the next and was little more than a royal inn; but more ambitious *tambos* at larger intervals actually required the support of villages, many of which were founded or rebuilt at the time of the Inca to meet this need. (Their original function is still preserved in the suffix *tambo* — the Hispanicized form — of these villages' names.) Of course, the mass of the peasantry did not have any occasion to use this network of highways; the only persons free to travel beyond the territory of their own community were the court officials, the *chasquis,* or those possessing special passes. Roadblocks to check travelers were set up outside the main cities.

The communities whose territory was traversed by the royal highways were obliged both to help build the stretch in their area and then to assure its maintenance. This was one of the many obligations, divided among the various *ayllus,* that made the gigantic public works of the Inca possible. The time given to the building of the highways, like that given to the temples or irrigation projects, was counted as part of the *mita,* the labor-tax "donated" to the emperor.

The desire to assure roads that were as similar as possible — despite the climatic, physical, and ethnic differences in the widespread territories — made it necessary to develop standards, dictated by the central government but put into application by local populations. This standard-

Pachacamac: A section of the upper terracing of the Temple of the Sun, erected by the Inca.

Pachacamac: Plan of the archaeological zone.
1 Temple of Pachacamac (pre-Inca oracle)
2 Temple of the Sun
3 Temple of the Moon

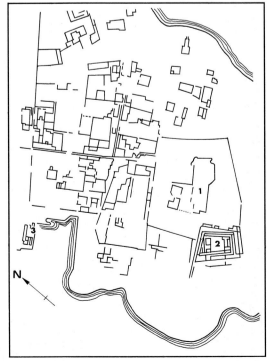

No province ever attempted to disturb them in
their own land, only seeking to be left in quiet
possession of their territories, and this seems to
me to have been a great advantage to the Inca.
There is no memory of such an attempt in
their registers; but after districts were reduced
to obedience, the great natural strength of this
region contributed to its security. The four
roads which diverge from Cuzco all are crossed
by rivers that cannot be forded at any time of
year, while the land is very rugged and
difficult. There cannot, therefore, be any
doubt that in this, and in possessing better discipline and more knowledge, lay the advantage
they had over all the other nations of this region. This superiority is shown in their
edifices, bridges, farms, systems of irrigation,
and in their higher moral lives.

POLO DE ONDEGARDO: *Report* (c. 1560)

Pachacamac: Remains of the pre-Inca temple,
seat of the oracle.

ization may be observed not only in the technical characteristics of the
roads, which — allowing for some adaptations to different circumstances — were similar throughout the Inca realm, but even in the
most ambitious and imaginative achievements of Inca engineering, the
bridges. Conceived by a people who did not have iron, the wheel, or the
arch, these bridges represent perhaps the maximum development of the
vegetal suspended bridge (a type also used in Southeast Asia).

The maintenance of these bridges was entrusted to the nearest *ayllu;* it
must have required highly specialized workers to replace the vegetal
elements — twisted fiber or vine cables up to sixteen inches in diameter
and up to 200 feet long. Two of these bridges, hailed by the chroniclers,
have been partially preserved — the stone elements, that is. The ruins of
the two pylons on a great bridge — built, according to Poma de Ayala, in
the time of Yahuar Huaca — are found at Pariabamba, on the Pampas
River, near the Inca city of Oranmarca. But it was the legendary bridge
over the Apurimac that remained in use up to the end of the nineteenth
century, one of the most celebrated of all Peruvian monuments. Built,
according to Garcilaso, by Inca Roca, it was situated in a strategic position
and permitted communication between the royal highway leading from
Cuzco to the north and the highway leading west to the coast.

George Squier, the great English traveler in Peru, visited the bridge
when it was still in use in 1864 and has left us its measurements: 150 feet
across, and at least 118 feet over the waters of the Apurimac River.
Access to the bridge was particularly arduous; the last stretch of highway,
to the left of the river, was carved out of solid rock for approximately 650
feet, receiving its light from a series of apertures facing the ravine. Two
platforms — the one on the Cuzco side being a natural one, made of
stone — supported the bastions, or piers, through which the ends of the
stretched cables were conducted. Garcilaso provides more details on this:
"Inserted under the bastion supporting the tower were five or six beams
the size of oxen and protruding at the ends, arranged one on top of the
other like a stairway. Each suspension cable was secured to a beam, so
that the bridge was drawn up tight and did not collapse under its own
great weight." This interesting arrangement — which the Spaniards replaced later with a capstan — solved the problem of the anchorage on
land of the *maguey* (an agavelike plant) fiber cords, "the size of a man."

In these extraordinary bridges, we find the original characteristics of
the Inca technical-architectural culture: the exceptional precision in the
use of materials — each subjected to a rational exploitation of its
capacities — reflected in the simplicity of design and in the flawless inser-
tion of the whole into the environment. And no less impressive than the
achievements in engineering at the Apurimac bridge was the nearby
oracle consecrated to the spirit of the river, which spoke through a
female idol, made of a tree trunk, to be found inside the hut, supplying
an interpretation of the ceaseless roar of the waters below. Whatever
their own accomplishments, the Inca never forgot their gods.

Closely connected to the Inca network of roads and bridges was their
system of fortifications. Now there was a partial defensive system that
served as protection for the various pre-Inca confederations. The major
pre-Inca system was that surrounding the Titicaca region, bearing witness to the defensive needs of the confederation of the Collas, whose
influence reached south into the northwest portion of Argentina. Mention has also been made of the systems that protected the Mochica and
Chimu states, based on the defense of the passes that provided links
between the valleys along the coast and the highlands, as well as through
passages along the seashore (Paramonga being merely the most notable
example). There is one fortress after another as far as Tumbez, all of
them along the upper highway, which continued as far as Colombia.

It was precisely along this natural line of communication that the Inca
built both the main route of their royal highway and the major line of
defensive forts. A group of fortresses not far from Cuzco, particularly to
the northeast, protects the capital from the menacing unknown in the
tropical forests to the east. Some of these structures — Ollantaytambo,
Pisac, Villcanota, Choquequirac — are the finest examples of the Inca art

Left and above:
Pachacamac: Two details of the construction
of the Temple of the Sun.

of fortification and demonstrate the complexity attained by architecture in the final century of their power. A similar strategic concept dictated the building of the fortresses that protected Quito from the northeast, practically serving as the capital of the northern part of the empire; these, too, are late works — Tuza, Lumichaga, Guaca — but follow the same basic pattern used elsewhere in the Inca defense network.

Technology and Architecture

It was precisely the need to coordinate both organization and construction with what was becoming this almost continental extension of the Inca state that turned their architecture toward simplified solutions, whether in the structures of monumental centers or their decorative motifs. The integration of man-made constructions with the natural landscape prevailed over the imposed geometry of architectural masses that had established an opposition between the works of man and nature ever since the time of the pan-Andean culture of Tiahuanaco. The Inca expended great care in developing a science of space, with the aim of controlling, by means of the "central locality" process, even the most remote communities of the immense territory tributary to them. But while there was only a slow shifting from the mysticism of space to territorial policies, the sacerdotal class was replaced at the head of the state machinery by the governor-bureaucrats and the military. One might even speak, in connection with the imperial policies of the Inca, of a progressive "proletarianization" of all the essential elements of the cultural and social life of the Andeans, with the aim of extending the basic political and economic unity to the furthermost corners of the empire. Simplification, integration, unification, then, did not necessarily add up to liberation for the mass of Andeans.

Perhaps it was the lack of writing that explains the unique development of regulation in the Inca Tahuantinsuyu, whether it was in the accounting system, the keeping of statistics, or the measurement of time and distance. And as we have seen, each of these systems easily coordinated with one another as well as with the radial structure of the state. The need for homogeneity constantly outweighed the desire for variety in the Inca world. The productions of the artisans in Cuzco, for example, although they did not decline in the purely technical sense, reveal — in comparison, that is, with the many-faceted cultural expressions that had previously flourished in the Andean world — a rigid typological structure leaving little leeway for improvisation or personal variants. This is particularly evident in products such as pottery and textiles.

The primary desire to reconcile the widespread areas of the empire with the flawless functioning of its organization had specific effects on architecture. The Inca, for instance, made extensive use of clay models for the representation of their monuments and their territory as well as for the actual planning of structures. To be sure, the Inca were drawing on a tradition from numerous Andean populations, notably those of the coast; in ceramics, beginning with the classical period, clay models of hutlike structures, dwellings of more than one story, and even temples were common from Salinar to Callejon de Huaras and Nazca. But the Inca's representation in miniature of landscape elements and monuments does not have the ritual significance that was found in these sporadic examples of the earlier times, buried in the *huacas* of dead ancestors. The Inca turned these models into technical aids, useful in the unswerving effort of imperial policies to control all things and to symbolically reduce them in size so as to have the entire empire at arm's reach — whether it was through the rigorous census-taking or by making models of the lands that had been colonized.

This reduction of different components to fit into one structure, entirely visible, was the source of the programmed planning of Cuzco (as we have seen), which itself was an authentic "model" of all the peoples and regions of the empire at large. Once again, it is Garcilaso who pins down the importance of this technique, describing most vividly the masterpiece

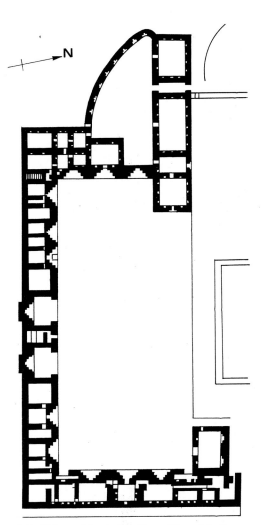

Lake Titicaca: Island of the Moon: Plan of the Convent of the Chosen Women.

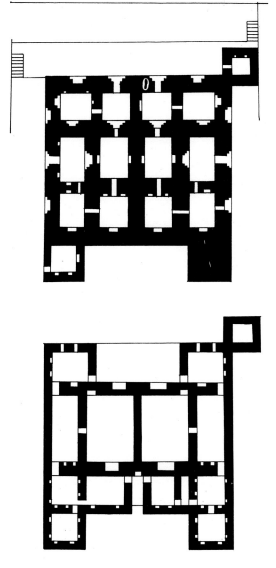

Lake Titicaca: Island of the Sun: Plan of the Palace of the Inca. Top: ground floor; bottom: second story.

of an obscure Cuzco artisan: the scale model of the city offered to the royal Spanish visitor, Damian de la Bandera:

"I myself saw the model of the city and of the province of Cuzco, patiently built of clay, pebbles, and twigs. In it one could clearly see the four main roads that branch out from Cuzco and head for the four confines of Peru. One sees, moreover, the entire city of Cuzco, with its large and small squares, its streets and alleys, the blocks with their houses, from the nearest to the most distant. A mere glance at this model filled you with the utmost astonishment. You felt the same wonder in observing the entire surrounding region, represented in equal detail. There were the mountains, hills, valleys, rivers, the torrents with their meanderings — in short, all of Cuzco, as not even the world's most able cosmographer could have drawn it."

Further testimony to the Inca's concern for scale reproduction of architectural elements is to be seen in the Kenko stone (page 167), the great boulder that has been turned into a model-sanctuary, and other similar works (page 127). The custom was extended, moreover, to the representation of natural elements, of plants and animals, no doubt to symbolize the absolute sway of the Inca over all things, almost as if it were a repetition of creation. Thus, according to Garcilaso once again, items fashioned in gold and silver for the garden of the Temple of the Sun in Cuzco included not only grain and plants but even firewood logs:

"Attached to each royal palace of ancient Peru were enormous gardens, adorned and perfumed by every plant and flower produced by nature, and it was into the coolness of these gardens that the emperor would descend for his daily walk. But set in among the trees and flowers were silver copies of the plants, flowers, and fruits, placed there by the Inca artisans. Using this same precious metal, they imitated to perfection the growth of the plant, the blossoming of the flower, and the ripening of the fruit. Among the other marvelous things they imitated, for example, was a maize plant, with the roots, stalk, leaves, ears, and all. The tassle that protrudes from the ear of maize was made entirely of spun gold, while the other parts from the roots up were made of silver.

"In these gardens, the Inca artisans also wrought domestic animals in both gold and silver, including rabbits, foxes, mice, toads, snakes, lizards, butterflies, and all sorts of birds, some of these latter resting on a branch, others with their wings spread or hanging from the corollas of flowers. They also adorned the gardens with reproductions of wild beasts, such as a puma, a boa constrictor, or a jaguar, giving each one the position most in keeping with its nature."

We have mentioned that the lack of writing — and, so far as is known, of materials such as paper and ink — in part explains the Inca's resorting to models. But this would hardly explain how the model, whether understood in the imitative sense or as a plan to be followed in building operations, had assumed such enormous importance in every area of Inca life. We must continue to search further in the Inca world.

A complementary feature of the simplicity of the architecture was the extreme refinement of technique achieved by Inca artisans in the building of stone walls. The walls of the main public buildings, of the dwellings of the emperor and his dignitaries, were erected with the same craftsmanship that was necessary to turn out the most laborious exemplars of the goldsmith's art, of fabrics, or of ceramics. Two aspects of this wall-building struck the fancy of the conquistadors and the chroniclers: the size of the blocks used, and the perfection of the joining, which was all but invisible. "It was impossible to introduce even the blade of a knife," they said then, and it can be said today: the Inca technique still deserves our admiration. This is especially so when we consider that the builders lacked iron and the stones had evidently to be shaped mainly with other stones.

Modern research, in fact, has not been able to explain all the procedures used in every phase of these walls, although Garcilaso is perhaps a reliable source. If nothing else, he mentioned the motives behind this painstaking care in dressing the stones. He says many times that the aim of this work was to deceive and astound anyone who might observe these

Moray: The agricultural terracing of the Inca reveals the "geometrization" of nature common throughout much of Andean culture. *(See back jacket.)*

Page 151:
Machu Picchu: Terracing and dwellings on the precipitous slope on the circumference of the city center.

Pages 152–153:
Machu Picchu: A general view of the city, and its spectacular setting, so remote and inaccessible that the Spaniards never found it and it remained to be discovered in 1911. On the peak to the far left of the open area is the *intihuatana* (page 104).

gigantic blocks, apparently joined so effortlessly. The almost flawless joining of the blocks ruled out the use of a mortar (and the Inca never did have a lime cement), although Garcilaso claims that in order to fit two surfaces more easily, a red slime called *hancac allpa* was used, which left no trace after drying. Garcilaso and Cieza de Leon also claim that a special lacquer made of silver, lead, and gold was often inserted between the blocks to make the edifice appear more opulent. This custom was said to have been the cause of the Spaniards' destroying so many buildings — for they were always looking for more valuable metals. Although this story is probably not true, it is significant that the chroniclers chose to credit it, for it is part of the unexplained mystery that hovers around the Inca technique of stone working.

We have established how deeply rooted in the creative experience of the Inca was the need to refer each and every object to be built to an external model, whether by reproducing it faithfully in another material or as a model of an original otherwise too large to manipulate. In either case, we can observe that the motive behind the reproduction was a desire to possess the object through its image. When applied to monumental architecture, particularly structures in stone, this attitude led on the one hand to the imitation, in the finished product, of a model of the project, while on the other hand it inspired an effort to imitate in gigantic undertakings the processes of nature itself, hidden as they usually are to the eyes of men.

The first of these observations leads us to admit the possibility that the highly distinctive style of joining blocks was derived from the study of clay models, in which the interstices between the stones do not depend on any actual need but merely obey the a priori and abstract rules of composition. In the clay model, the junctures between blocks served no real function but were designed — i.e., traced on the clay surface — after the model was completed. As a result, the "stonework" could be arranged at will, on a purely aesthetic basis: the paramount desire was to avoid pure perpendicular and parallel lines. This same aesthetic principle seems to have been at work in most of the great stone structures, and such a principle seems to be the only way to explain the extreme plasticity of the great blocks, which seem to have adapted themselves to one another through time and through a tremendous force of compression. The other need — that of imitating the work of nature — stems, then, from the fear of a rebellion of the object so shaped against its human creator.

The mythical elaborations used by the Inca imperial family — to demonstrate their own divine descent and their perfect harmony with the world of nature — also involved these very structures. They had to appear to have been built not by man but by the gods — at least by the emperor as a deified being. Added to the emperors' desire of evoking astonishment, therefore, was the still more fundamental one of hiding their human nature, through the work of stone-dressers so refined as to remove virtually all traces of the effort involved. Even in the dimensions of the stones, the camouflaging with nature reaches such a point that Garcilaso himself, in considering the great stones at the Sacsahuamán fortress, claimed they could not have been brought there from some other locality: instead of recognizing the labor involved, he pays tribute to the patience that made it possible for men to fit together stones already found in the area. In fact, all Inca structures involved, even in the elements that appear most coarse, a completely human manipulation of the stone.

This concept, which distinctly subordinates the total mass of the edifice to the material used, so as to remove all static moments and rigid elements, could be carried out only with the use of exceptional technical means. It is not enough to say that the blocks were tirelessly rubbed together to achieve a perfect adherence and a perfect junction; we must also imagine an *ideal* prior to the actual designing, and one then reproduced with millimetric precision. This then suggests that the plans for the empire's most majestic undertakings — the great public buildings, the Sun temples, the palaces of the emperors — were all worked out with the utmost care in Cuzco by the royal architects before they were constructed

Left:
On this peak rising above the ceremonial area was the observatory with its *intihuatana,* an elaborate sundial. At the foot of the stairway leading up to it are the remains of two of the city's more ambitious buildings (the one on the right being the "temple of the three windows," pages 156–157); they were constructed with a more refined stonework, while the common buildings and terracing were built with irregular stones.

Above:
Machu Picchu: The main gateway of the city, along the long access stairway.

Machu Picchu: A view from below of the "temple of the three windows" and the adjacent terraces.

on their sites. Full-scale levies of thousands of men also had to be organized, while the construction — which must have lasted several years — was supervised by officials of the emperor who stood by with their detailed models.

Various classification systems have been proposed for the different types of Inca stone walls, according to their dimensions, the form of the blocks, the treatment of their surfaces, etc. Thus, the walls at Sacsahuamán have been classed as "cyclopean," while walls made of smaller stones with a greater finishing of the surfaces and more rigorously carved shapes are known as "polygonal"; walls made of still smaller stones, but

Page 158:
Machu Picchu: The stone channels and basins for collecting water within the city.

Page 159:
Machu Picchu: This entrance to a burial
chamber, dug into the rock beneath "The
Tower," reveals the sensitivity with which the
Inca fitted man-made elements with the
natural rock.

irregularly arranged, are classed as "cellular" by this system. But it is not necessary to get bogged down in such classifications. What is important is to realize that the different construction techniques do not represent a chronological progression — as was originally thought — but were used simultaneously, at least in the final century of Inca power, when most of their surviving structures were built. If there is a hierarchy involved, in fact, it has to do rather with the fact that the greater the religious, political, or military importance of a building, the greater care was taken in the stonework.

The indefinite variety in the cutting of the stone blocks, the dimen-

sional relationships within a single wall, the alternation in one and the same building of several "styles" — all these factors should not be studied on the basis of arid classification systems but primarily in relation to the specific role taken by each stone in the overall structure of an edifice. Each of the architects assigned to the great projects, whether the religious buildings, the fortresses, or the palaces, resolved the challenges in his own way, leaving the stamp of an unmistakable style not only on the structure as a whole but also on the individual stonework details.

Above:
Machu Picchu: View of "The Tower" (*El Torreón*), a sacred building with curved and inclined walls.

Great Inca Sanctuaries

If Cuzco was the political center of the Inca empire, where Manco Capac and his sister-wife had settled to establish the "navel" of the Tahuantinsuyu, then the Island of the Sun in Lake Titicaca represented the place where the Inca stock had originated (although, as we have seen, there were several conflicting origin myths). This island might be considered the gigantic *intihuatana* of the Inca world, the point where intercourse between the fecundating sun and the earth had taken place, and where it continued to do so in ritual. According to this particular legend, the first rays of the sun, after a great deluge, had fallen on this island and its surrounding lake. This tradition on the origin of the Inca dynasty

Right:
Machu Picchu: "The Tower" and (on the left) the so-called Palace of the Princess.

Machu Picchu: A grindstone used for grains, still in its original position.

pointed to the island as the place where the Sun had sent his children, the progenitors of the Inca people.

On the Island of the Sun, which had been painstakingly transformed into a vast garden through various terraces, priests cultivated the sacred seeds of maize; the harvest, symbol of the perennial fertility of the land, was annually distributed among all the empire's sanctuaries. Even the nearby Island of the Moon, or Coati, was considered sacred. And these two islands still contain the remains of two important monuments, known respectively as "Palace of the Inca" and "Temple of the Moon."

The Palace of the Inca is a small, two-story building, fifty by forty-four feet, rigorously symmetrical in all its subdivisions. The twelve rectangular spaces of the interior, for instance, were grouped so as to form two "apartments" of four rooms and two of two rooms. The front has two central portals, flanked by two niche-style false doors. All the apertures present the characteristics of the traditional trapezoidal tapering, familiar from many of the earlier Andean structures. On the upper story, subdivided into chambers of various sizes, a panoramic terrace overlooks the front and establishes communication between the two wings of the edifice. One might almost call it a "classical" building.

On the Island of the Moon, meanwhile, are the remains of a more extensive complex, called the Temple of the Moon but more likely an *acclahuasi,* a house for "chosen women," or a convent for the women consecrated to temple service. The building was laid out in the form of a U on three sides of a rectangular court (about 185 by 80 feet), opened to the north. Around this court were thirty-five rooms, some opening directly onto the main area, some connecting only indirectly or with an outer enclosure. This latter was used as a corral for the llamas or vicuñas that supplied the wool to be spun and woven by the Chosen Women. Of particular refinement was the external decoration of the courtyard walls — architectural motifs of stucco, with bordered and indented panels — while the entire building was painted yellow and red.

Both the Palace of the Inca and the Temple of the Moon bear witness not only to the fact that the Inca architects were mindful of the structural traditions of the land of the Collas but also, and above all, of the historical continuity between the culture of Tiahuanaco — centered near Lake Titicaca — and that of Cuzco. The relationship of these two sacred buildings (formerly surrounded by terraces and impressive gardens) with the total natural environment, was a compositional tradition that the Inca would exploit to the fullest.

If the Titicaca-Tiahuanaco region had the force of tradition in Inca life, a much more immediate and active ceremonial center was Pachacamac, on the coast just northwest of Cuzco. This, too, had been an important sacred site long before the emergence of the Inca; the ancient sanctuary at Pachacamac had been consecrated to a deity of that name, and he was worshiped by peoples up and down the coast. As the Inca empire incorporated these regions and their inhabitants, they also built their own great pyramid-temple at the site, dedicating it to the Sun and at once overwhelming the older sanctuary and absorbing the god Pachacamac. The Inca Temple of the Sun was built on a natural rise on one corner of the sanctuary enclosure; quadrangular in shape, it rose by five platform-steps to a height of seventy-five feet, with stairways connecting the various levels. It was painted a bright red and was visible for an even greater distance than the gaily painted sanctuary of old — thus serving as both a landmark for travelers on land or sea and announcing to all that the Inca's deity had superseded the old gods.

The faithfulness to archaic models and the absence in much of the sacred architecture of any stone decoration, by the way, has meant that the ruins of many Inca buildings have been difficult to identify — particularly, too, because of the disappearance of the wooden parts (partitions, beams, etc.) and the vegetal roofs. Furthermore, the removal by the Spaniards and other marauders of the decorations and elements of precious metals, which often formed an integral part of a building, although it may now render the perfection of the stonework more evident, has deprived the various rooms of almost all indications of their original

An Acclahuasi, *or "Convent of the Chosen Women," watched over by the "mother superior."*

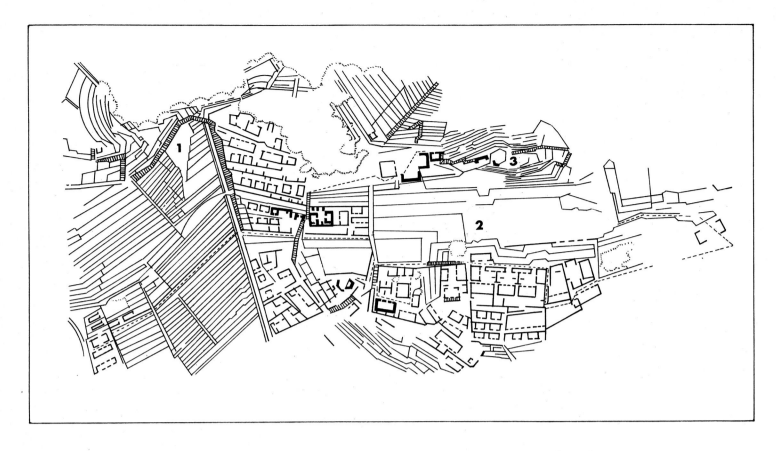

functions. This has often made it difficult for modern students to be precise about many of the Inca buildings — even in knowing to which god a temple was dedicated.

There are often, too, discrepancies between the traditional historical sources and modern archaeological conclusions, as is the case with the famed Viracocha Temple at San Pablo de Cacha, on the outskirts of Cuzco. According to tradition, the temple-sanctuary was built by the Emperor Viracocha to honor the god Viracocha, who had appeared to him predicting his victory over the Chancas; this would place the temple back about 1430. Yet archaeologists believe it dates from the last phase of the Inca period — almost a century later. In any case, it was a massive structure, over 300 feet long and about 90 feet high; its interior was divided by a thick wall that ran the length of the temple and probably carried the weight of the roof. According to the reconstruction of the nineteenth-century Englishman, Squier, the two "naves" of the interior were each divided by a median row of twelve columns (only one of which still stands), which supported the crossbeams of a ceiling. With its various attendant structures, it must have been a most impressive sanctuary.

Machu Picchu: General plan
1 Stairway up into the city
2 Open ceremonial area
3 Solar observatory with intihuatana

Machu Picchu

But of all the Inca sites, none has so caught the imagination of modern peoples as the city of Machu Picchu, which sits perched on the top of a rugged spur, covered with lush vegetation, looking out over the deep valley of the Urubamba River several hundred feet below. The fact that this center, which arose in the last period of the Inca power, did not get into the traditional histories and thus became "lost" — only to be rediscovered by Hiram Bingham in 1911 — has aided in leaving its structures as the best preserved in all the highlands. On the other hand, Machu Picchu cannot be taken as a typical example of Andean-Inca cities; it is an extreme development of the adaptability of Inca architecture to adverse environmental conditions.

Machu Picchu: A view through one of the apertures of the "temple of the three windows." The lower section was carved out of one of the enormous monoliths that make up the building's supporting walls.

Left:
Machu Picchu: View from below of the "temple of the three windows."

Right:
Kenko: This large natural stone formation over a cavern on the outskirts of Cuzco was carved to represent a model, or miniature, sanctuary. It is believed to be the burial site of the Emperor Pachacuti. Visible just to the left is a ceremonial open area.

Following pages:
Tambo Machay: The so-called Inca's Bath, a site near Cuzco that made use of a natural spring with medicinal waters.

The town rests on a narrow ridge, steep and craggy on every side, overlooked by the sharp bulk of Mount Huayna Picchu, which acts as a backdrop to the city as it is viewed from the approach side. A long twisting stairway of one hundred steps climbs along the crest after having passed through the access portal; this doorway itself is an imposing two-story structure, with its tapered opening. At the farthest part of the spur, in a natural depression, was a vast ceremonial space, of irregular perimeter and levels, while carved out of the rock overlooking this was the *intihuatana,* or solar observatory (still perfectly preserved). All the structures are of a clear granite, treated in accordance with the various Inca masonry techniques, from the coarsest sort for terracing to the kind that was accurately dressed and joined for the main public buildings.

One especially common technique at Machu Picchu is the inclination of the upper part of walls toward the interior of structures, thus "echoing" the shape of the sloping roofs. But such a device was part of a series of variants in the architectural elements of the same building and of different buildings, variants that are an organic characteristic of Inca design. Pure forms are rarely used by themselves, in isolation; as a rule, they condition one another, undergoing changes in parts and adapting themselves to particular situations or details. As a result, the buildings are rarely perfectly rectangular: at Machu Picchu as in the other mountain towns, the trapezoidal and other irregular forms prevail. Yet these little variants and irregularities should not be thought of as merely aesthetically determined. Thus, the peglike protuberances carved on the upper stone surfaces were used to secure the cord that held down the vegetal roofs, a most elegant solution to the functional and aesthetic problem of joining the two elements.

Quite aside from the demands made by construction techniques, the shape of the buildings and open places of Machu Picchu were in har-

mony with one of the most paramount characteristics of Inca monuments: the continuity between nature and the artifacts of man. The living rock itself was considered building material, and huge blocks were grafted onto it as if they were its organic continuation. In some cases, such as in the *intihuatana* (page 104) or the celebrated entrance to an underground chamber in the form of a stairway (page 159), it is the apparent freedom from all geometric schematism that makes the rocky material appear to share a vitality similar to that stamped into the great walls.

Even the succession of stone pools built at different levels on the slope and connected by stone canals appears to reproduce, with a brilliant display of technical expertise, not so much a work clearly built by the hand of man, as the reproduction in crystalline forms of a natural element: a stream flowing down the hill with successive waterfalls and tiny pools (page 158). The "sacred pool," indeed, was a recurrent feature in the architecture of other Andean towns; indications are that it had both an agricultural function (irrigation of cultivated land) and a ceremonial function (the exaltation of the emperor as, among other roles, the master of waters). A similar series of stone canals descending from terrace to terrace is to be seen at Tambo Machay, near Cuzco (pages 168–69).

Finally, beyond such details of structure, the city of Machu Picchu was planned as a transformation of nature into a human artifact, and this was achieved through the terracing. The whole city is surrounded by earthworks made with the utmost care, so that the buildings end up forming superimposed, parallel terraced masses along the slopes. It is more than integration; it is truly a symbiosis between the work of man and the natural setting. There is perhaps only one other Inca site that makes it quite so clear up to what point the transformation of the land for man's ends can blend in with nature. This is at Moray (page 149), in a valley that runs alongside and then merges with the Urubamba, where are to be seen the most eye-filling achievements in terracing — three vast hollows,

Ollantaytambo: The series of terraces that linked the lower part of the city to the majestic fortress.

Ollantaytambo: A view of the five terrace walls that comprise the upper fortress; the fifth tier, with the trapezoidal niches, is clearly identifiable, while above that rises the uppermost ceremonial area.

Ollantaytambo: The wall with the niches and the monumental gateway leading to the top of the fortress.

artificially made, with concentric step-terraces, all arranged like some gigantic funnel or amphitheater. The Moray terraces were for agricultural purposes, but they reveal how indistinct was the difference for the Inca between the preparation of land for farming and for civic life.

The Urubamba Valley contains many other significant Inca centers, each of which throws light on some particular aspect of urban life and the architecture of the last period, immediately before the Conquest. Near Machu Picchu, for instance, the towns of Vinay Huayna and Inti Pata present similar structures, with baths, stairways, and terraces. Notable at Vinay Huayna is the semicircular tower like that at Machu Picchu (page 160), built with blocks that tapered off gradually toward the top, also with a sharp inclination, and also with the trapezoidal windows.

Ollantaytambo

In the Yucay River valley northwest of Cuzco sits Ollantaytambo, a complex of buildings that includes a small residential center and a majestic defensive structure. This latter, consisting of five terraces that rise to a massive (but unfinished) structure on the summit, belonged to the final period of Inca power; some would say that the Ollantaytambo fortress represents the climax of Inca stonework techniques. The sequence of steep terraces connected by a stairway, was in keeping with the Inca concept of strategy, which we have already seen at Paramonga and at Sacsahuamán. At Ollantaytambo, however, there is an even more precise relationship between the position of the various terraces and the masonry techniques used, due not so much to strategic needs as to the hierarchical concept that conferred an ever greater importance on the buildings as they approached the more sacred area at the peak of a hill. And, indeed, we may note a progressive transformation in the stonework, from the supporting walls at the bottom to the six great blocks at the summit.

In the sequence of five terraces which comprise the best preserved part of Ollantaytambo, we have, starting at the bottom, a polygonal wall of blocks of only moderate size, virtually uniform in their dimensions, arranged in fairly distinct rows, although not always horizontally. The second terrace is similarly constructed, but the blocks are appreciably larger. Great stones reinforce the corners, and here and there the rough alignment into rows is disrupted by the use of more distinctly polygonal blocks. The third tier is held up by a wall with slightly larger components alternating with smaller ones, sometimes arranged in rows but mainly irregular. The fourth terrace reveals a more orderly arrangement, with large polygonal blocks flanked by small stones, and all put together with great care.

It is the fifth tier where the "soft" technique of dressing stone attains its most grandiose and consummate stage. The enormous boulders are handled with an exceptional lightness, and many possess the characteristic protuberances — possibly left over from the processing of the stone, possibly used to fix accessory elements to the walls — which produce an aesthetic effect that appeals to us today. This fifth tier also includes two special features. One is the section of wall with large trapezoidal niches; evidently this was built by following a quite detailed plan, including the use of "prefabricated" boulders: the niches were made by alternating stones of simple trapezoidal lines with others having a small protruding element on top, a joining technique derived from that used with wood.

The other remarkable element of this fifth tier is the majestic portal (page 172) which leads to the sacred area of the uppermost tier. This portal demonstrates the most sophisticated handling of the plastic adaptation of the stone to its form and function. The trapezoidal outline is broken horizontally into two parts, the top half simulating the motion of a door being turned, while all the elements — including the small protuberances — combine to create a totally unified architectural element.

Messenger:
I was there with all the army,
I was sleeping at the joining of the Queru,
I was concealed in the sides of Yana-huara.
In that valley are many woods
In which to make an ambuscade.
I was there in a house,
for three days and nights,
Concealed in that ravine;
There I felt cold and shivering.
Rumi Nahui came there and told his plan:
"You shall go at night,
While I return to my place.
In the Tambo they have a great Raimi festival,
And all will be very drunk.
Then come at night
With the army of Cuzco."
So saying, he returned,
And we stood there all that night.
That day was one of watching,
A day of gazing at the sun.
Ollantay passed it,
And his men were drinking,
And he with his men,
For three days.
In the middle of the night,
Without anyone speaking,
We rushed into the Tambo.
The men were not seen by those outside.
It was like the lightning.
Fear fell upon them,
They were caught in a net.
As they drank, they were seized.
We sought for Ollantay;
He too was in the net.
Rumi Nahui was there;
We found him still sick.
. . . .
All were conquered.
Almost a hundred thousand were prisoners.
The women followed near,
All of them weeping.

Ollantay (III:2)

At the very top of the hill lie numerous stone blocks, some of them of immense proportions, semi-dressed and to all appearances ready for the completion of what was perhaps to have been the most breathtaking masterpiece of all Inca architecture. Six of them, deservedly world-famous, make an almost vertical wall thirteen feet high; these six are not joined directly to one another but have five thin slabs of stone inserted between their interstices. These monoliths alone are sufficient to establish that the structure was to have been the palpable expression of an architectural concept representing a new departure from that of the other buildings of the final Inca period. As with the portal at the fifth tier, the Inca's usual sensitivity to the inner potential of the material has evolved to the point of envisioning a genuine possibility of expressing motion. At least it transformed the wall, which might have remained inert, into an artifice in which the colossal elements were no longer put together in accord with some surface texture but as though obeying some internal logic of a mysterious mechanism. The enormous mass of the wall, in which the interstices between the main blocks were not hidden but treated in such a way as to appear to be natural folds or joints in a creation of exquisite woodwork, presents a surface in which the irregularities were made to dovetail. No line is absolutely straight; on the contrary, the slight curve of the interstices is one of the main reasons for an effect of an impeccable finish and compactness, leaving the impression of a reciprocal adaptation between the two parts.

The great wall at Ollantaytambo, in other words, was achieved with the criteria of the artisan, "hand-made" and anti-symmetrical, a work in which the identification of the craftsman with his material attained a primitive dimension that shook off architectural inertia — the goal being precisely that of creating a perfection more typical of nature than of the works of man. The wall seems not to have been built but to have sprung up spontaneously: even the enormous size of the monoliths drives from our imagination all the relationships of normal building techniques. It appears to aim at an extreme harmonization of the organizing role of the state with the disintegrating forces of nature.

It is as if the door whose upper half swings open and the wall that can expand and contract represent an abortive bid by the Inca to erect a monument to the impending end of the world, to some apocalyptic earthquake in which the works of man themselves, surging with rebellion, would have regained the upper hand forever over the supreme force of domination — nature. Of course, it was not to be. And as a result, the great wall at Ollantaytambo represents in its unfinished state both the zenith of Inca culture and the fact that it was soon to be toppled to its nadir by foreign forces. The spirit of the ancient *huacas* had failed.

Following page:
Ollantaytambo: The six monoliths on the uppermost open area — the remains of a construction that, even though unfinished, is considered the most majestic monument of the final period of Inca culture.